120 Celebration
Cross Stitch Cards

Gillian Souter

David and Charles

A DAVID & CHARLES BOOK
David & Charles is a subsidiary of F+W (UK) Ltd.,
an F+W Publications Inc. company

First published in the UK in 2005

Distributed in North America
by F+W Publications, Inc.
4700 East Galbraith Road
Cincinnati, OH 45236
1-800-289-0963

ISBN 0 7153 1911 6
Designed by Off the Shelf Publishing
and printed in Singapore by KHL Printing Co Pte Ltd.
for David & Charles
Brunel House   Newton Abbot   Devon

Executive Editor Cheryl Brown
Editor Jennifer Proverbs
Executive Art Editor Alison Myer
Art Editor Prudence Rogers
Production Controller Ros Napper

Gillian Souter is the author of some twenty-five books, including craft titles for
both children and adults; her last book was the popular *Cute & Cuddly Cross Stitch*.
Gillian was born in Scotland, moved to Australia when young, and now lives in
a beautiful coastal village in New South Wales.

David & Charles books are available from all good bookshops; alternatively you can contact
our Orderline on (0)1626 334555 or write to us at FREEPOST EX2 110,
David & Charles Direct, Newton Abbot, TQ12 4ZZ (no stamp required UK mainland).
Visit our website at www.davidandcharles.co.uk

CONTENTS

INTRODUCTION

Cards and cross stitching strike me as a marriage made in craft heaven. For a keen cross stitcher (and what cross stitcher isn't keen?), it's a chance to create small, portable projects that turn scraps of fabric and threads into cherished keepsakes marking special occasions for people you love. For me, this book was also an opportunity to think a little about all those occasions – from the cradle to the grave – and add a personal touch to the way they might be celebrated.

Say it with Cross Stitch

I first took up cross stitching to make an elaborate sampler celebrating my first nephew's birth. Then along came another nephew, then a niece, then a close friend's baby, and so on, until I realized that I'd have to choose smaller projects or become a social recluse. A nice compromise to welcome a new baby is a cross stitch card, and if you can add baby's name, all the better.

Engagements and weddings are obvious events worth marking with a handmade card, particularly as the choice of shop-bought cards can seem a little impersonal. Major birthdays and anniversaries positively demand stitching attention. A stitched card is perfect for Mother's Day and a nice idea for Father's Day (but he still deserves that pair of socks). After that, it's up to you what's card-worthy. If you're a manic stitcher, cards are a great way to occupy your fingers between major projects. Many of the general birthday cards could be stitched to have on hand for when a friend's birthday comes around. Some of the Christmas designs are quite intricate and are only viable in quantity if you've been stitching earlier in the year.

Card Formats

The simplest style of card is a single-fold card. Fabric that has been cross stitched can be fringed and simply attached to the front with double-sided tape. The alternative is to mount the work in a double-fold card, which conceals the raw edges of the fabric and frames the design nicely in a window. The shape of the card can vary, although it needs to have one straight edge along the fold.

A huge variety of pre-cut cards is available from craft shops or you can order direct from the suppliers listed on page 103. Almost all of the projects in this book specify a card size available from one of these suppliers. If you are planning to buy pre-cut cards, it's helpful to first obtain the supplier's catalogue, which lists all of the card sizes, window shapes and sizes, and colours and card weight. If necessary, adapt pre-cut mounts to fit by cutting a window larger or by adding a double mount.

It's less expensive and very satisfying to cut your own cards for displaying your work. You can buy large sheets of card from art and craft shops and then divide this up to make a number of double-fold cards. Instructions for this appear on page 97, followed by tips on mounting the cross stitched fabric in the card and adding a decorative touch.

A single-fold card (below) and a double-fold card offer two ways of turning cross stitch into a greetings card.

The window in a double-fold card can be any shape you choose. If you can't find a shape to suit your design, cut your own.

There are lots of other ideas for decorating the finished cards scattered throughout the projects and a short overview appears on page 99.

Gift Ideas

Sometimes a cross stitch card is a complete gift in itself. However, if you're seeking ideas for a small gift to complement the card, I've included a few suggestions at the end of each chapter. Of course, there are unlimited ways you can use cross stitch motifs to adorn personal or household items, but these may give you a little inspiration.

Some of the gift ideas in this book require general and simple sewing techniques such as hemming, seaming and edging with bias binding. You might want to refer to a general guide to sewing if your technique is a little rusty.

A handful of cards require custom-made windows; templates for these appear on page 102.

Tags

When you don't have a lot of time on your hands, a gift tag can be a good alternative to a card. These mini motifs really are a great way to use up snippets of fabric and can be quickly stuck on a small piece of card with double-sided tape. Write your message on the back of the tag and attach it to a gift with a length of ribbon or string.

There are a dozen or so tag ideas in this book, but you might be tempted to design your own; if you're stuck for inspiration, try adapting a motif from one of the larger card designs.

Make it Yours

Some of the designs in this book have a space for you to add the name or age of the recipient using the alphabets and numbers that are charted on pages 100–101. If there isn't space among the stitching, a few words in gold or silver pen on the card frame could add a personal touch.

Get Stitching!

Complete stitching instructions can be found on pages 94–95 but for experienced stitchers, here are four things to note before you begin:

* DMC stranded cottons (floss) have been used to stitch the samples throughout this book; a conversion chart for those who wish to use Anchor appears on page 104.
* Stitch all the projects using two strands for cross stitch and a single strand for backstitch and french knots, unless the instructions specify otherwise.
* A quick way to work with two strands is to cut a long single strand, thread both ends through the needle and catch the end loop at the back on your first stitch to neatly secure the end and form a double strand.
* Feel free to use fabric other than the one suggested, although if it's a different count, you might need to change the size of the card window.

A Year of Celebrations

Around the world and around the year, people find ways to celebrate together. Whether it be a day to mark your culture, a religious festival, or an occasion to enjoy family ties, make it even more special with a cross stitch card.

A New Year

A Date to Remember

Easter

Religious Celebrations

Mother's Day

Father's Day

Hallowe'en

Time of Plenty

Christmas

Gift Ideas

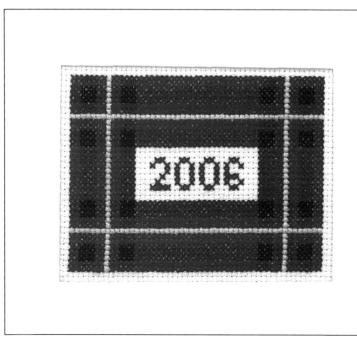

NEW YEAR TAG

☐	726
☐	996
☐	3340

backstitch:

☒	3837

New Year Tag

Stitch the tag design on a 3½ x 2in (9 x 5cm) piece of white 14-count Aida. Trim to within three bands of the design and stick onto a 3½ x 2in (9 x 5cm) piece of blue card. Snip off two corners and cut a slot for ribbon tie.

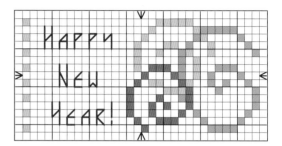

Hogmanay

This Scottish celebration of the new year deserves a tartan tribute.

* Cream 14-count Aida, 5 x 4in (12 x 10cm)
* DMC stranded cottons (floss) as listed in the key
* Cream double-fold card with a 3¾ x 2¾in (9.5 x 6.5cm) rectangular window

DESIGN SIZE   3¾ x 2½in (9.5 x 6.5cm)

NOTES   Stitch the relevant year, following the number chart on page 101.

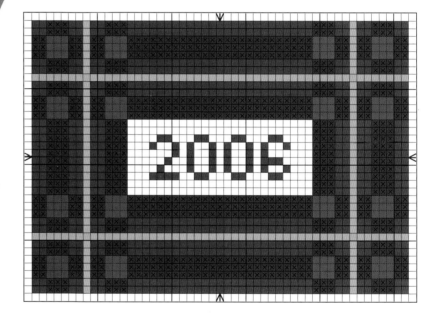

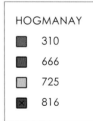

HOGMANAY

■	310
■	666
☐	725
☒	816

Chinese New Year

Celebrate with a dancing dragon.

* White 14-count Aida, 4 x 5in (10 x 12cm)
* DMC stranded cottons (floss) as listed in the key
* Green double-fold card with a 2¼ x 3in
  (6 x 7.5cm) rectangular window

DESIGN SIZE   1¾ x 3in (4.7 x 7.8cm)

TO FINISH   Glue on some gold leaves for good luck!

CHINESE NEW YEAR	
■	310
▨	444
■	666
⊠	905
□	907
⊙	blanc
backstitch:	
⧄	666

ROSH HASHANAH	
■	310
▨	725
■	798
■	817
□	910
▨	946
backstitch:	
⧄	310

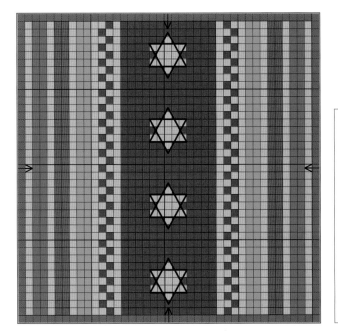

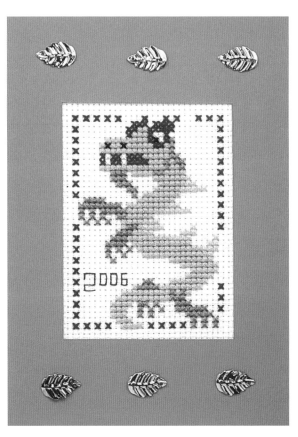

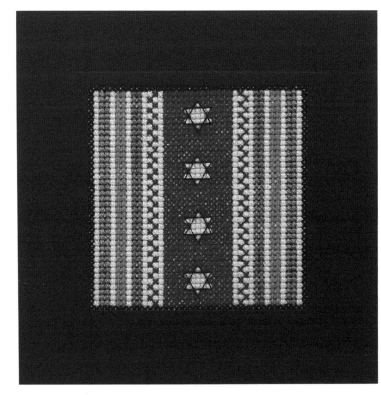

Rosh Hashanah

Stitch this for the Jewish New Year.

* White 14-count Aida, 4 x 4in (10 x 10cm)
* DMC stranded cottons (floss) as listed in the key
* Black double-fold card with a 3 x 3in
  (7.5 x 7.5cm) square window

DESIGN SIZE   3 x 3in (7.5 x 7.5cm)

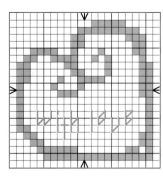

HEART TAG	
▧	972
backstitch:	
☑	972

Heart Tag

Stitch the tag design on a 2½in (7cm) square of red 14-count Aida. Trim around the design and stick it onto a square of yellow card.

Valentine's Day

Get all sentimental with this heart-warming scene.

* White 28-count evenweave, 5 x 5in (12 x 12cm)
* DMC stranded cottons (floss) as listed in the key
* Red double-fold card with a 3¾in (9.5cm) round window

Design Size 3¼ x 3in (8 x 7.5cm)

To Finish Arrange heart-shaped sequins around the window and glue them in place.

Gift Idea Page 26 features a matching gift.

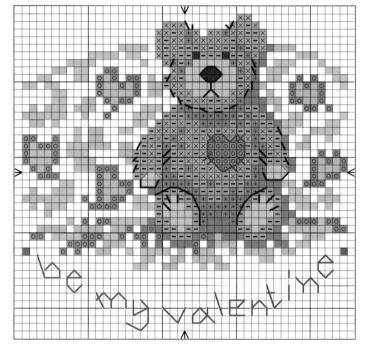

VALENTINE'S DAY					
▨	451	⊠	3827	backstitch:	
◉	760	■	3831	☑	898
▢	761	⊞	3853	☑	3831
■	898	⊟	3854		
▢	954	▢	3855		
▢	3755				

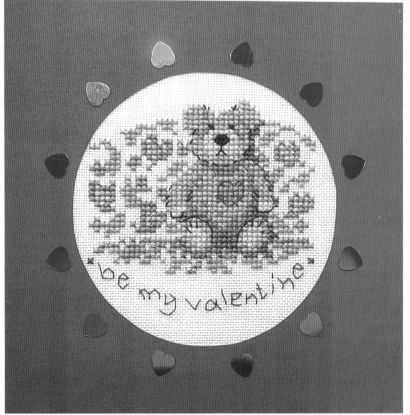

St Patrick's Day

Mark the day with a bold Celtic knot.

* Cream 14-count Aida, 4½ x 4½in (11 x 11cm)
* DMC stranded cottons (floss) as listed in key
* Green double-fold card with a 3¼in (8.3cm) round window

DESIGN SIZE   2¾ x 2¾in (7 x 7cm)

TO FINISH   Outline the window with gold pen.

ST PATRICK'S DAY	
⊠	699
⊙	700
⊟	702
▢	704
backstitch:	
⧄	5284

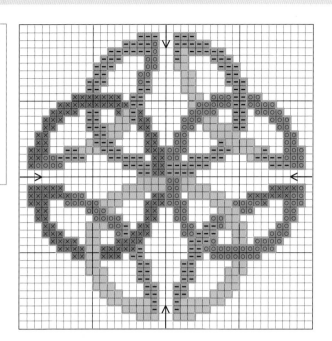

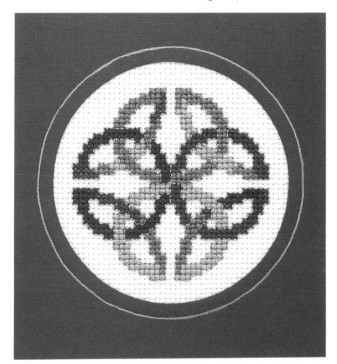

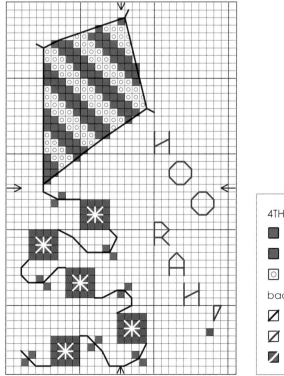

Fourth of July

Celebrate the day with a free-flying kite.

* White 14-count Aida, 4 x 5in (10 x 12.5cm)
* DMC stranded cottons (floss) as listed in the key
* Red double-fold card with a 2½ x 3¾in (6.5 x 9.5cm) rectangular window

DESIGN SIZE   2 x 3⅜in (5 x 8.5cm)

4TH OF JULY	
■	666
■	792
⊙	blanc
backstitch:	
⧄	310
⧄	792
◪	blanc

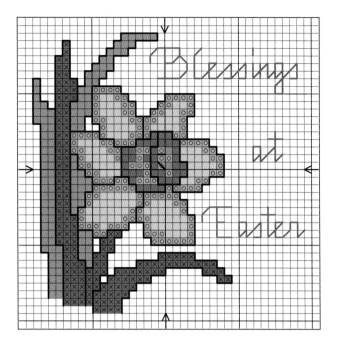

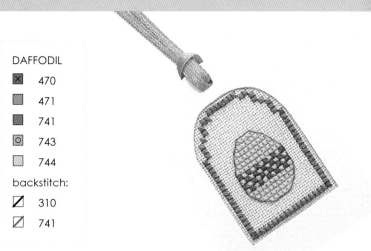

DAFFODIL

☒	470
▧	471
▦	741
◉	743
░	744

backstitch:

◪	310
◪	741

Easter Bunny

Send Easter greetings with this bouncy rabbit.

* White 28-count evenweave, 4 x 5in (10 x 12cm)
* DMC stranded cottons (floss) as listed in the key
* Pink double-fold card with a 3¼ x 4in (8 x 10cm) oval window

DESIGN SIZE   3¼ x 4in (8 x 10cm)

Daffodil

Here's a card to celebrate the spirit of Easter.

* White 14-count Aida, 5 x 5in (12 x 12cm)
* DMC stranded cottons (floss) as listed in the key
* Ivory double-fold card with a 3in (7.6cm) square window

DESIGN SIZE   2¾ x 2¾in (7 x 7cm)

Chick & Eggs

Warm a heart with this Easter design, which comes complete with a gift tag.

* Yellow 28-count evenweave, 5 x 5in (12 x 12cm)
* DMC stranded cottons (floss) as listed in the key
* Sunflower double-fold card with a 3in (7.6cm) square window

Design Size 2⁷/₈ x 2⁷/₈in (7 x 7cm)

Tag Stitch the large egg design on a 2½ x 3in (6 x 7.5cm) piece of yellow 28-count evenweave. Use the pattern on page 102 to cut two card sections, one with an aperture, and mount the work between them.

Gift Idea See page 26 for a gift idea featuring the tag design.

EASTER BUNNY

▦	472		backstitch:
▦	738	⊘	413
▦	760	⊘	3328
◎	963		french knots:
⊕	blanc	●	413
		●	3328

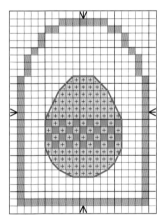

CHICK & EGGS

▦	340		backstitch:
▦	471	⊘	721
▦	721	⊘	3799
⊕	726		french knots:
☐	727	●	3799

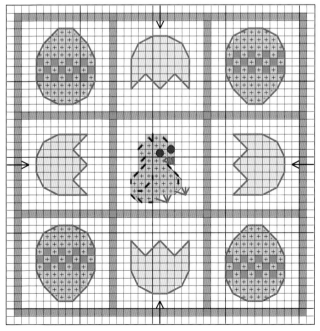

Id Ul-fitr

At the end of Ramadan, Muslims celebrate the festival of Id Ul-fitr. Here's a lovely design based on an Islamic mosaic.

* Grey 28-count evenweave, 4 x 4in (10 x 10cm)
* DMC stranded cottons (floss) as listed in the key
* Silver double-fold card with a 3 x 3in (7.5 x 7.5cm) square window

DESIGN SIZE   2¾ x 2¾in (6.6 x 6.6cm)

Id Mubarak Tag

'Id Mubarak' is the traditional greeting given during Id Ul-fitr. Stitch the tag design on a 3½in (9cm) square of dark blue 14-count Aida. Mount it in a pale blue double-fold card with a 2⅜in (6cm) round window.

ID MUBARAK TAG	
◙	blanc
backstitch:	
▧	762

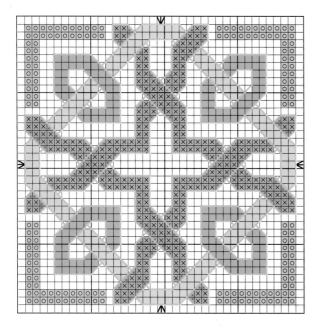

ID UL-FITR	
☐	955
◙	964
⊠	996
▥	3846
backstitch:	
▧	5283

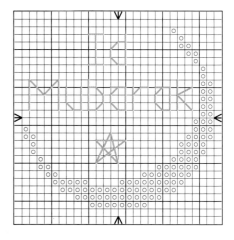

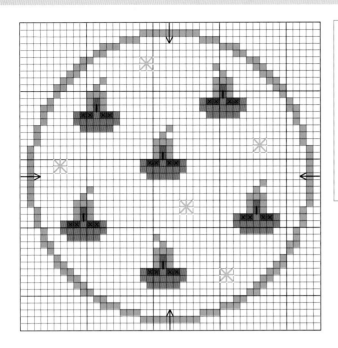

DIWALI	
■	606
■	972
⊠	975
▥	976
backstitch:	
⧄	310
⧄	5284

Diwali

During the Hindu festival of light, homes are decorated with small lamps called 'diwas'.

* Black 14-count Aida, 5 x 5in (12 x 12cm)
* DMC stranded cottons (floss) as listed in the key
* Gold double-fold card with a 3³∕₈in (8.5cm) round window

DESIGN SIZE 3 x 3in (7.5 x 7.5cm)

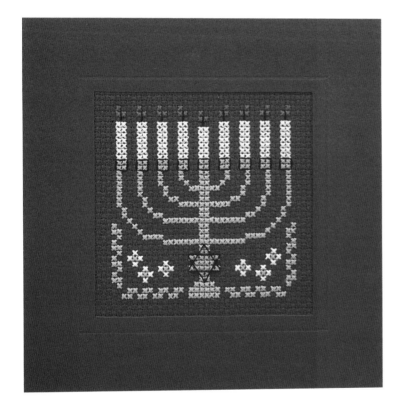

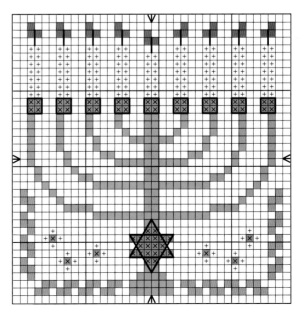

Hannukah

Celebrate the Jewish Festival of Lights.

* Green 14-count Aida, 4 x 4in (10 x 10cm)
* DMC stranded cottons (floss) as listed in the key
* Green double-fold card with a 3 x 3in (7.5 x 7.5cm) square window

DESIGN SIZE 2½ x 2½in (6.5 x 6.5cm)

HANNUKAH	
■	608
■	728
⊠	742
▥	907
⊞	blanc
backstitch:	
⧄	310

Mother's Day

Flowers are always right for this occasion.

* White 14-count Aida, 4 x 6in (10 x 15cm)
* DMC stranded cottons (floss) as listed in the key
* Red double-fold card with a 2¾ x 4½in (7 x 11.5cm) rectangular window

DESIGN SIZE   2¼ x 4½in (5.7 x 11.5cm)

GIFT IDEA   See page 27 for a gift to match this card.

POPPIES	
■	349
⊠	351
▦	352
◉	470
▨	471
■	3021
▢	3855
backstitch:	
⬚	349

ROSEBUDS	
▦	703
◉	987
⊠	3706
▨	3708
backstitch:	
⬚	816

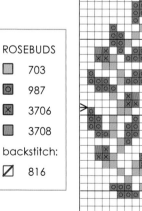

Rosebuds Tag

Stitch the design on a 4in (10cm) square of cream 14-count Aida. Mount in a pale green double-fold card with a 2¾in (7cm) round window.

Dad's Day Off

Father's Day is a time for dad to put the paws up.

* Peach 28-count evenweave, 4½ x 4½in (12 x 12cm)
* DMC stranded cottons (floss) as listed in the key
* Sunflower double-fold card with a 3½in (9cm) round window

DESIGN SIZE 2¾ x 2⅞in (6.6 x 7cm)

TO MOUNT Add a double mount in a contrasting colour.

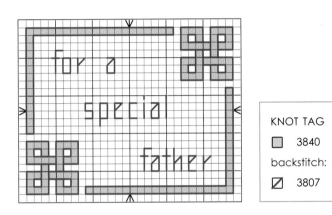

KNOT TAG	
☐	3840
backstitch:	
☑	3807

DAD'S DAY OFF			
■	352	◯	3865
⊍	402	＋	blanc
■	535	backstitch:	
⊟	744	☑	535
☐	745	french knots:	
☒	3756	■	535
☐	3840		

Knot Tag

Stitch the tag design on a 5 x 4in (11 x 9cm) piece of white 14-count Aida. Trim around the stitching, fringe a row and stick it on a 3½ x 3in (9 x 7.5cm) rectangular window.

Pumpkin Tag

Stitch the tag design on a 3½ x 3in (9 x 7cm) piece of black 28-count evenweave. Mount it in an orange double-fold card with a 2¼ x 1¼in (5.7 x 3cm) rectangular window or trim and stick it on a simple tag.

GIFT IDEA See page 26 for a gift featuring this design.

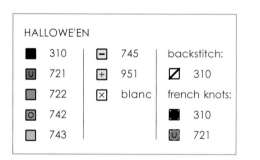

HALLOWE'EN

■	310	⊟	745	backstitch:	
U	721	⊞	951	⧄	310
▦	722	☒	blanc	french knots:	
◉	742			■	310
▨	743			U	721

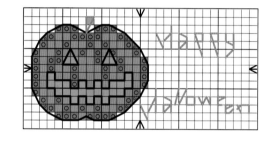

PUMPKIN TAG	
▦	702
◉	721
▦	722
▦	972
backstitch:	
⧄	310
⧄	702
⧄	972

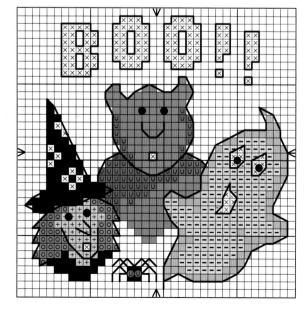

Hallowe'en

Greet your best friend with this terrifying trio.

* Apricot 14-count Aida, 4 x 4in (10 x 10cm)
* DMC stranded cottons (floss) as listed in the key
* Black double-fold card with a 3 x 3in (7.5 x 7.5cm) square window

DESIGN SIZE 2½ x 2½in (6.5 x 6.5cm)

TO FINISH The mount has been decorated with moon-shaped sequins; you could draw these on with a gold pen.

HARVEST BASKET

	307		608		3340
	349		704		3819
	350		721	backstitch:
	552		722		838
	553		906		

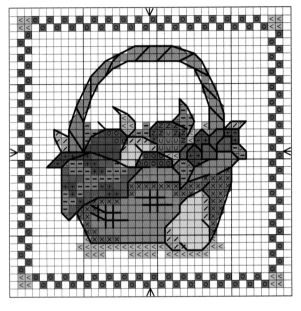

THANKSGIVING

	451
	606
	741
	3348
	3799
	3853
	3854
	3863
	blanc
backstitch:	
	310
	606
french knots:	
	310

Thanksgiving

This turkey's going incognito for the occasion.

* Coffee 28-count evenweave, 4 x 4in (10 x 10cm)
* DMC stranded cottons (floss) as listed in the key
* Chocolate double-fold card with a 2¾in (7cm) square window

DESIGN SIZE 2½ x 2¼in (6 x 5.7cm)

Harvest Basket

Stitch a charming basket of autumn fruit.

* Cream 28-count evenweave, 4 x 4in (10 x 10cm)
* DMC stranded cottons (floss) as listed in the key
* Ivory double-fold card with a 2¾in (7cm) square window

DESIGN SIZE 2⅝ x 2⅝in (6.5 x 6.5cm)

Snowmen

A single snowman would make a fun tag.

* Red 14-count Aida, 5 x 5in (12 x 12cm)
* DMC stranded cottons (floss) as listed in the key
* Pearl double-fold card with a 3⅝in (9cm) round window

DESIGN SIZE 3⅛ x 3⅛in (7.7 x 7.7cm)

Season's Greetings

Three motifs in vibrant colours.

* White 14-count Aida, 5 x 4in (12 x 10cm)
* DMC stranded cottons (floss) as listed in the key
* Turquoise double-fold card with a 3¼ x 2½in (8 x 6cm) rectangular window

DESIGN SIZE 3 x 1⅞in (7.3 x 4.7cm)

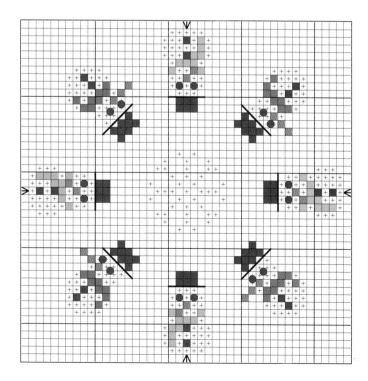

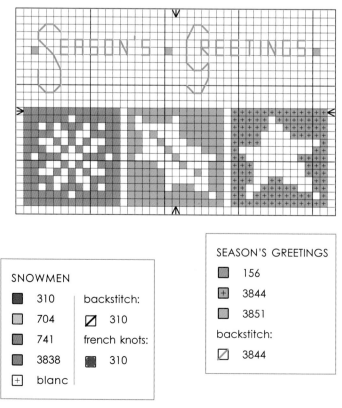

SNOWMEN		
■	310	
■	704	backstitch:
■	741	◩ 310
■	3838	french knots:
⊞	blanc	■ 310

SEASON'S GREETINGS	
■	156
⊞	3844
■	3851
	backstitch:
◩	3844

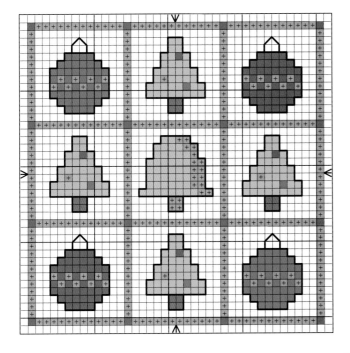

Christmas Baubles

Tree decorations make a cheery card.

* Green 14-count Aida, 4 x 4in (10 x 10cm)
* DMC stranded cottons (floss) as listed in the key
* Ruby double-fold card with a 3 x 3in (7.5 x 7.5cm) square window

DESIGN SIZE 2⅞ x 2⅞in (7 x 7cm)

GIFT IDEA See page 27 for a gift to match this card.

CHRISTMAS BAUBLES			
■	435	■	798
■	666	+	972
■	703	backstitch:	
■	725	◿	310

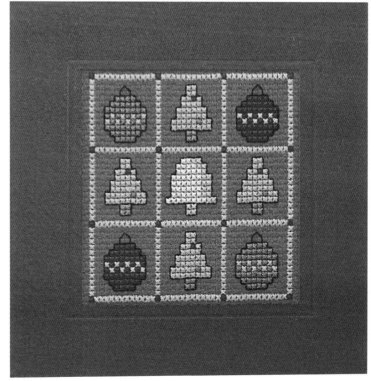

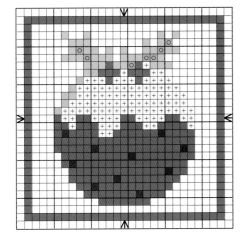

PUDDING TAG	
■	301
■	310
□	453
■	606
◉	702
□	704
+	blanc

Pudding Tag

Stitch the design on a 3in (7.5cm) square of grey 14-count Aida. Mount it in a green double-fold card with a 2¼in (5.5cm) square window.

Angel

An angel heralds the festive season.

* Blue-grey 28-count evenweave, 4 x 5in (10 x 12.5cm)
* DMC stranded cottons (floss) as listed in the key
* Gold double-fold card with a 3 x 4in (8 x 10cm) oval window

DESIGN SIZE   3⅜ x 1⅞in (8.4 x 4.7cm)

TO FINISH   Stitch small beads onto the fabric before mounting.

ANGEL					
■	728	⊡	948	▨	728
▫	745	⊞	3865	▨	3810
⊟	747	backstitch:		french knots:	
■	807	▨	535	▨	3810

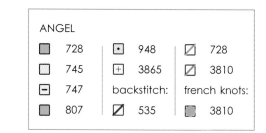

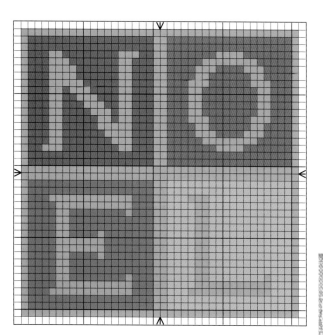

Nöel

Rich colours make this design a gem to stitch.

* White 14-count Aida, 4 x 4in (10 x 10cm)
* DMC stranded cottons (floss) as listed in the key
* Gold double-fold card with a 3 x 3in (7.5 x 7.5cm) square window

DESIGN SIZE   2⅞ x 2⅞in (7 x 7cm)

NÖEL	
■	350
■	553
▫	703
▫	728
■	3838

Good Tidings

Send messages of hope at this special time.

* Beige 28-count evenweave
* DMC stranded cottons (floss) as listed in the combined key
* Coloured two-panel card

DESIGN SIZE   FULL DESIGN - 3¼ x 4¾in (8.2 x 11.5cm)

JOY - 2 x 1¾in (5 x 4cm)

LOVE - 2¾ x 1¾in (7 x 4cm)

PEACE - 3¼ x 1¾in (8.2 x 4cm)

To FINISH Trim ½in (1cm) around the stitched design and remove two threads from each edge. Stick the work onto a two-panel card using double-sided tape.

GIFT IDEA Frame the full design as a festive sampler, as shown on page 27.

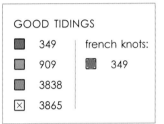

GOOD TIDINGS		
▨ 349	french knots:	
▨ 909	▨ 349	
▨ 3838		
⊠ 3865		

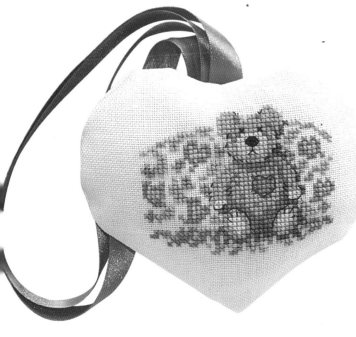

Scented Heart

Make this hanging heart for anyone dear to you.

* White 28-count evenweave, 7 x 12in (17.5 x 30cm)
* DMC stranded cottons (floss) as listed in the key
* Polyester stuffing
* Lavender; ribbon

1 Cut the fabric in half. On one piece, stitch the design following the chart and key on page 10, and omitting the text.

2 Trace the heart on page 102 and cut a paper template. Position this on the back of the stitching and mark around it.

3 Place the fabric pieces together, right sides facing. Sew around the marked line, leaving a gap for turning. Trim ½in (1cm) around the seam, clip the curves and turn right side out. Wrap stuffing around the lavender and push it in the heart.

4 Handsew the opening closed. Cut two 20in (50cm) lengths of ribbon; fold and sew them onto the back of the heart.

Egg Cosy

An egg-cellent gift at Easter or any time of year.

* Yellow 28-count evenweave, 9 x 4in (22 x 19cm)
* DMC stranded cottons (floss) as listed in the key
* Thick flannel, 9 x 4in (22 x 19cm)

1 Cut the evenweave in two 4½ x 4in (11 x 9.5cm) pieces and stitch the egg design on each, following the chart and key on page 13.

2 Trace the pattern on page 102 and cut out a paper template. Use this to shape the evenweave. Cut two matching pieces from the flannel.

3 Sew the two evenweave pieces together with a ³⁄₈in (1cm) seam around the curved edge. Sew the flannel pieces together likewise.

4 Turn the outside section and insert the flannel section. Turn the raw edges in by ³⁄₈in (1cm) and sew the sections together.

Treat Bag

At Hallowe'en, treat a child to this sweet sack.

* Black 28-count evenweave, 6 x 10½in (15 x 26cm)
* DMC stranded cottons (floss) as listed in the key
* Black lining fabric, 6 x 10½in (15 x 26cm)
* Black ribbon or fabric tape

1 Cut the fabric in half. On one piece stitch the pumpkin design, following the chart and key on page 18. Stitch a decorative border, 1in (2.5cm) in from each edge.

2 Place the two fabric pieces together, right sides facing, and sew a ½in (1cm) seam along the sides and base. Turn right side out.

3 Fold the lining in half and seam the sides. Fit this in the evenweave bag and turn in both openings by ½in (1.5cm).

4 Cut an 8in (20cm) length of ribbon and pin the ends between the inner and outer bags to form a handle. Sew around the opening of the bag to finish.

Festive Sampler

These messages are worth reading all through the year.

* Beige 28-count evenweave, 5 x 6in (13 x 15cm)
* DMC stranded cottons (floss) as listed in the key
* Cream card for a mount (optional)
* A wooden frame with an opening at least 4 x 5in (10 x 12.5cm)

1 Stitch the design following the chart and key on page 25.

2 Paint the frame a warm red and allow to dry. Sand with medium sandpaper, wipe off the dust and then apply a coat of semi-gloss varnish.

3 If the size of the frame allows it, cut a mount of cream card to fit the design and lay it in the frame.

4 Cut stiff white card to fit inside the frame. Lay this on the back of the stitched fabric, fold the edges over and tape them onto the back. Fit into the frame.

Tree Decorations

A set of these is a perfect stocking-filler.

* Silver or gold 14-count perforated paper
* DMC stranded cottons (floss) as listed in the key

1 Following the chart and key on page 21, stitch individual grid squares with space around each one.
Stitch two for each double-sided decoration and trim two squares around each motif.

2 Form a hanging loop of six-stranded cotton (floss), securing ends in the back stitching of one section.

3 Tape the two sections together, wrong sides facing, with double-sided tape.

Bookmark

A book is a wonderful gift, especially when accompanied by a handmade bookmark.

* White 14-count Aida, 4 x 6in (10 x 15cm)
* DMC stranded cottons (floss) as listed in the key
* Red card, 2½ x 6in (6.5 x 15cm)
* Narrow ribbon

1 Stitch the design following the chart and key on page 16, omitting the text and the top-left poppy and its stem.

2 Trim to within four thread blocks of the design and then fringe one block at each edge. Use double-sided tape to affix the stitched piece to the card.

3 Make a small cut near the base of the card. Thread a narrow ribbon through and secure it with an overhand knot. Trim the ends.

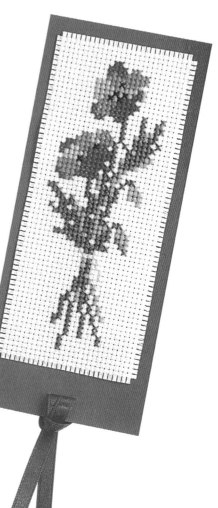

FOR BABIES & CHILDREN

The birth of a baby is always a special occasion and deserves a card that has been lovingly stitched. In fact, the whole of childhood is dotted with events worth marking and occasions to be celebrated in cross stitch.

BIRTH CONGRATULATIONS

TWINS & MORE

NAMING BABY

BABY'S FIRST

SCHOOL DAYS

STEPS IN LIFE

BIRTHDAY BOYS

BIRTHDAY GIRLS

GIFT IDEAS

Baby Bears

This cute design for a new baby comes in traditional colour schemes for girls and boys; or you could choose your own combination.

* White 28-count evenweave, 5 x 5in (12 x 12cm)
* DMC stranded cottons (floss) as listed in the key
* Pastel double-fold card with a 4in (10cm) square window

DESIGN SIZE 3½ x 3½in (9 x 9cm)

TO FINISH Rule a border line around the window of the card with a gold or silver pen.

BABY BEAR		BOY	GIRL
⊟	211	⊙ 156	760
■	535	☐ 3747	963
▦	738	backstitch:	
☐	772	◿ 156	760
☐	3078	◿ 535	535
		french knots:	
		■ 535	535

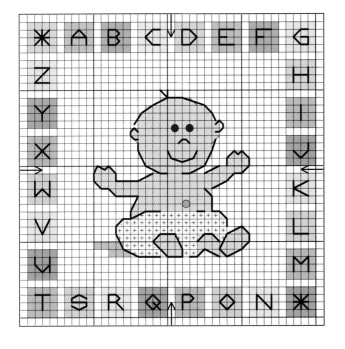

Alphabet Baby

You might prefer to personalize this design by spelling out baby's name on the blocks.

* White 26-count evenweave, 4 x 4in (10 x 10cm)
* DMC stranded cottons (floss) as listed in the key
* Salmon double-fold card with a 3in (7.6cm) square window

DESIGN SIZE   3 x 3in (7.5 x 7.5cm)

GIFT IDEA   See page 46 for a gift to match this card.

ALPHABET BABY		
341	backstitch:	
772	3799	
744	french knots:	
948	3799	
3824	3824	
blanc		

RATTLE TAG	BOY	GIRL
553	3843	603
554	996	605
744		
backstitch:		
553	3843	603
743		
french knots:		
743		

Rattle Tag

Choose your colour scheme and stitch the tag design on a 3¼ x 2in (8 x 5cm) piece of white 14-count Aida. Fit it in a double fold tag with a 2½ x 1in (6 x 3cm) window, or trim and stick it on a small piece of card. The lilac colour scheme is pictured on page 28.

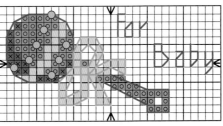

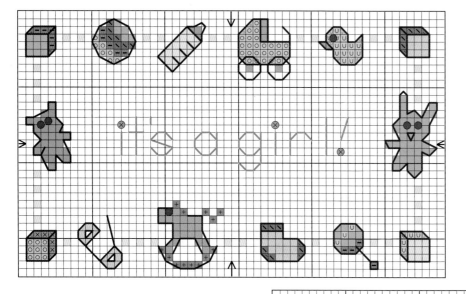

HELLO BABY!

☐	153	☐	3825
+	209	S	3853
☒	597	**backstitch:**	
U	726	◪	413
☐	727	◪	562
−	760	◪	597
☐	761	**french knots:**	
◪	793	●	413
☐	3348	●	562
☐	3747	☒	597
◎	3811		

Hello Baby!

Here are two designs you could stitch before baby is even named.

* White 28-count evenweave, 6 x 4in (15 x 10cm)
* DMC stranded cottons (floss) as listed in the key
* Parchment double-fold card with a 4½ x 3in (11 x 7cm) square window

DESIGN SIZE   4 x 2³⁄₈in (10 x 6cm)

PERSONALIZE   Stitch a design and add the gender when baby arrives.

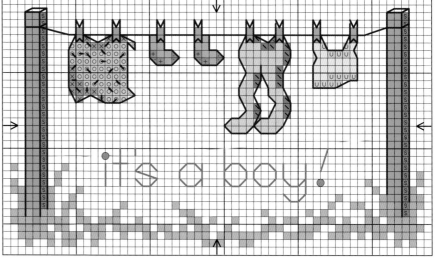

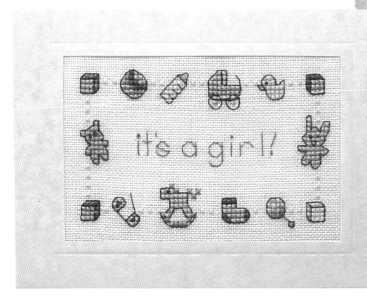

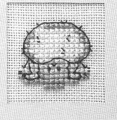

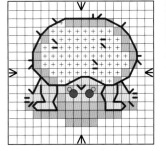

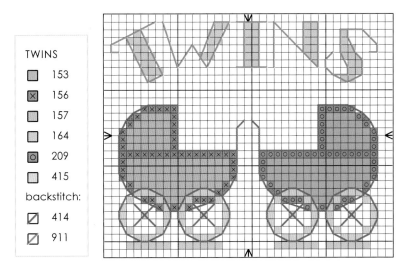

BOTTOMS UP

◎	353	⊞	blanc
▨	453	backstitch:	
▨	743	▨	535
▨	948	french knots:	
▨	3348	▪	535

Twins

Double the trouble, double the joy.

* Grey-green 28-count evenweave, 4 x 4in (10 x 10cm)
* DMC stranded cottons (floss) as listed in the key
* Lilac double-fold card with a 3⅜in (8.3cm) circular window

DESIGN SIZE   2⅝ x 2¼in (6.5 x 5.5cm)

Bottoms Up

Stitch as many babies as needed!

* Peach 28-count evenweave as required
* DMC stranded cottons (floss) as listed in the key
* Peach double-fold card without window

DESIGN SIZE   1 x 1in (2.5 x 2.5cm) each

TO MOUNT   Cut windows measuring 1½in (3.5cm) square to frame each stitched design.

TAG   A single baby would make a delightful tag.

TWINS		
▨	153	
⊠	156	
▨	157	
▨	164	
◎	209	
▨	415	
backstitch:		
▨	414	
▨	911	

Baby Sampler

Welcome to the animal kingdom!

* White 14-count Aida, 5 x 5in (12 x 12cm)
* DMC stranded cottons (floss) as listed in the key
* Ivory double-fold card with a 4in (10cm) square window

DESIGN SIZE 3¾ x 3¾in (9.5 x 9.5cm)

PERSONALIZE Use the alphabet chart on page 100.

TO FINISH Cut dots with a hole punch and stick on.

TAG Stitch a single motif on Aida, fringe the edges and stick on a square of coloured card.

GIFT IDEA See page 46.

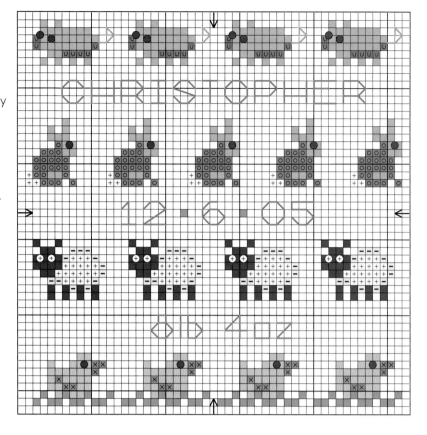

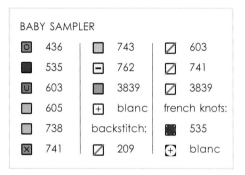

BABY SAMPLER

⊙	436	▨	743	▱	603		
■	535	⊟	762	▱	741		
U	603	■	3839	▱	3839		
▢	605	⊕	blanc	french knots:			
▢	738	backstitch:		■	535		
✕	741	▱	209	⊕	blanc		

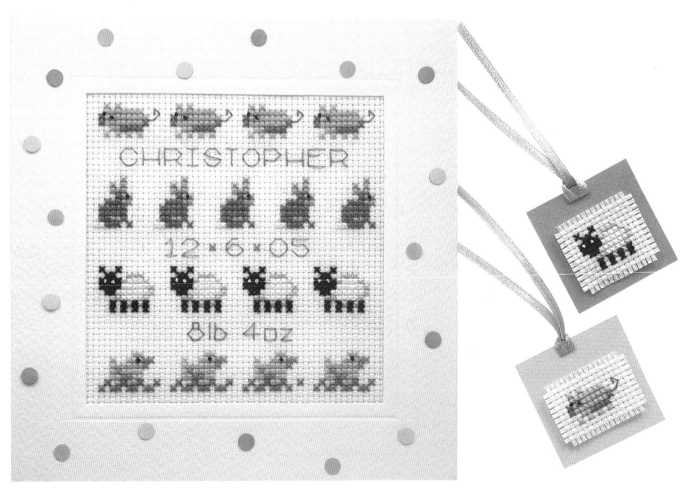

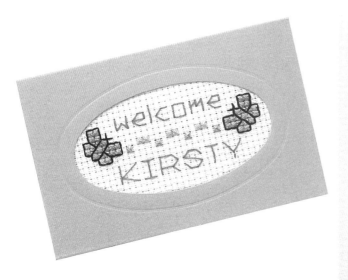

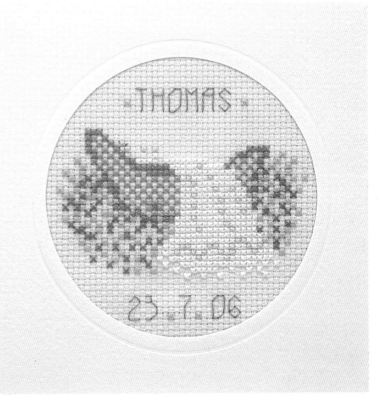

Welcome Tag

Stitch the tag design on a 3¼ x 2in (8 x 5cm) piece of white 14-count Aida. The alphabet is charted on page 100. Fit it in a double-fold tag with a 2½ x 1¼in (6.5 x 3cm) oval window, or trim and stick it on a small piece of card.

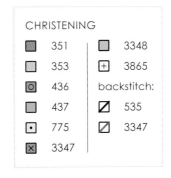

WELCOME TAG

☐	341	backstitch:	
☐	3609	◩	310
☐	3854	◩	3851

Christening

Stitch this for a christening or just to welcome the new baby.

* Yellow 14-count Aida, 5 x 5in (12 x 12cm)
* DMC stranded cottons (floss) as listed in the key
* Ivory double-fold card with a 3½in (9cm) round window

DESIGN SIZE   3¼ x 3in (8.5 x 7.5cm)

PERSONALIZE   Use the alphabet chart on page 100.

CHRISTENING

☐	351	☐	3348
☐	353	⊞	3865
⊙	436	backstitch:	
☐	437	◩	535
•	775	◩	3347
☒	3347		

FIRST BIRTHDAY

▨	318
☐	726
☐	996
☐	3819
▨	3825
⊠	3843
⊙	3853

backstitch:

◪	310
◪	3843

french knots:

▪	310

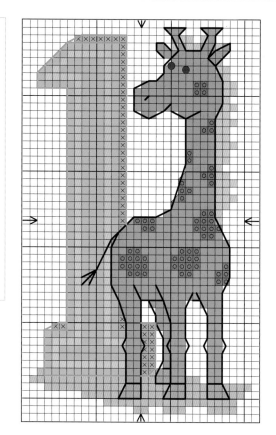

First Birthday

A first birthday is a gigantic event.

* White 14-count Aida, 4 x 6in (10 x 15cm)
* DMC stranded cottons (floss) as listed in the key
* Yellow double-fold card with a 2¾ x 4½in (7 x 11.5cm) rectangular window

DESIGN SIZE 2¼ x 3¼in (5.5 x 9.5cm)

TO FINISH Cut and stick a blue double mount inside the window before mounting the cross stitch.

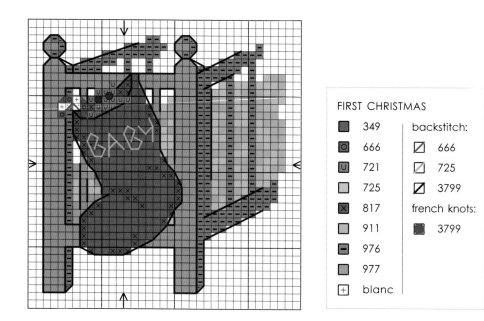

FIRST CHRISTMAS

■	349	backstitch:		
⊙	666	◪	666
∪	721	◪	725
☐	725	◪	3799
⊠	817	french knots:		
☐	911	▪	3799
⊟	976		
☐	977		
⊞	blanc		

Tooth Fairy

Mark the arrival of the first tooth!

* White 28-count evenweave, 4 x 4in (10 x 10cm)
* DMC stranded cottons (floss) as listed in the key
* Silver double-fold card with a 3in (7.5cm) square window

DESIGN SIZE 2⅝ x 2⅝in (6.5 x 6.5cm).

PERSONALIZE Stitch the date of the first tooth loss.

GIFT IDEA See page 47 for a gift to match.

TOOTH FAIRY

□	157		backstitch:
□	369	◪	535
□	744	◪	760
⊠	760		french knots:
□	761	◼	535
□	948		
⊞	blanc		

First Christmas

A baby in the house makes for a special Christmas.

* Navy 14-count Aida, 5 x 5in (12 x 12cm)
* DMC stranded cottons (floss) as listed in the key
* Gold double-fold card with a 3⅜in (8.3cm) round window

DESIGN SIZE 2½ x 2½in (6 x 6cm)

Starting School

Heading off to school is a big adventure.

* Grey-green 28-count evenweave, 5 x 4in (12 x 10cm)
* DMC stranded cottons (floss) as listed in the key
* Sky double-fold card with a 4 x 3in (10 x 8cm)
  oval opening

DESIGN SIZE   3⅝ x 3in (9 x 7cm)

STARTING SCHOOL

☐	745	backstitch:	
☒	955	▨	798
◉	958	▨	3799
☐	959	french knots:	
☐	3348	▨	798
■	3799	▨	3799
⊞	blanc		

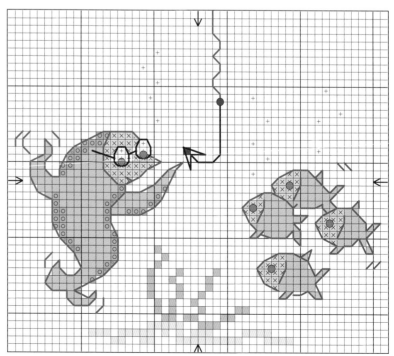

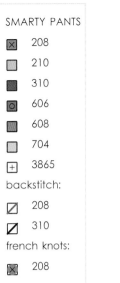

SMARTY PANTS	
☒	208
▫	210
▪	310
◉	606
▨	608
☐	704
⊞	3865
backstitch:	
◪	208
◪	310
french knots:	
☒	208

Smarty Pants

A good test result deserves suitable recognition.

* White 14-count Aida, 4 x 4in (10 x 10cm)
* DMC stranded cottons (floss) as listed in the key
* Lilac double-fold card with a 3in (7.5cm) square window

DESIGN SIZE 2⅝ x 2⅝in (6.5 x 6.5cm).

TO FINISH Draw chicken footprints on the mount with a silver pen.

GIFT IDEA See page 47 for a matching gift.

Prize Cup

Stitch this one for a little champion.

* White 28-count evenweave, 5 x 5in (12 x 12cm)
* DMC stranded cottons (floss) as listed in the key
* Cobalt double-fold card with a 3⅜in (8.3cm) round window

DESIGN SIZE 2½ x 2½in (6 x 6cm).

PRIZE CUP	
☒	156
◉	414
▫	415
☐	3753
⊞	blanc
backstitch:	
◪	792
◪	3799

Confirmation

Welcome a child into the Church with this card.

* White 14-count Aida, 4 x 4in (10 x 10cm)
* DMC stranded cottons (floss) as listed in the key
* Pale grey double-fold card with a 3in (7.5cm) round opening

DESIGN SIZE   2⅝ x 2⅝in (6.7 x 6.7cm)

TO FINISH   Add a pretty ribbon.

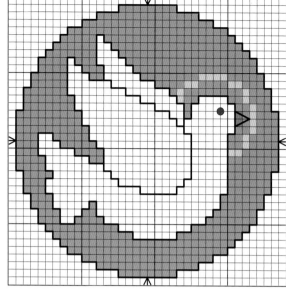

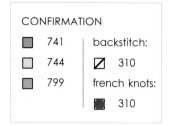

CONFIRMATION		
▨ 741	backstitch:	
☐ 744	◩	310
▨ 799	french knots:	
	◼	310

Bar Mitzvah

Jewish children take part in this ceremony to mark the start of religious life.

* Cream 14-count Aida, 4 x 3in (10 x 8cm)
* DMC stranded cottons (floss) as listed in the key
* Ivory double-fold card with a 3 x 2in (8 x 5cm) oval window

DESIGN SIZE   2¼ x 1¾in (5.7 x 4cm)

NOTE   For a girl, change the text to 'Bat Mitzvah'.

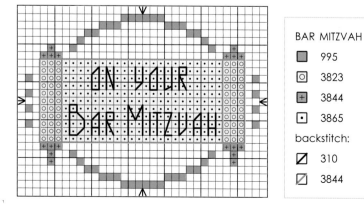

BAR MITZVAH	
▣	995
◉	3823
⊞	3844
·	3865
backstitch:	
◩	310
◩	3844

Congratulations!

Stitch a little encouragement.

* White 14-count Aida, 4 x 4in (10 x 10cm)
* DMC stranded cottons (floss) as listed in the key
* Cobalt double-fold card with a 3in (7.5cm) square window

DESIGN SIZE 2⅝ x 2¾in (6.5 x 7cm)

CONGRATULATIONS!		
☒ 317	backstitch:	
▢ 318	◩ 310	
▢ 703	◩ 703	
▢ 726	◩ 726	
▢ 798	◩ 798	
▢ 3801	◩ 3801	

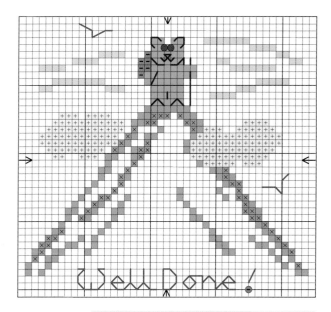

WELL DONE!		
⊞ 3756	☒ 3848	◩ 3781
⊟ 3765	▢ 3849	french knots:
▢ 3811	backstitch:	⊟ 3765
▢ 3827	◩ 3765	◼ 3781

Well Done!

Mark a success with this brave bear.

* Blue 14-count Aida, 4 x 5in (10 x 12cm)
* DMC stranded cottons (floss) as listed in the key
* Sky double-fold card with a 3⅛ x 4in (8 x 10cm) oval window

DESIGN SIZE 3 x 2¾in (7.5 x 7cm)

Helicopter

Every young boy dreams of flying his own helicopter.

* Blue 14-count Aida, 6 x 4in (15 x 10cm)
* DMC stranded cottons (floss) as listed in the key
* Blue double-fold card with a 4½ x 2⁷⁄₈in (11 x 7cm) rectangular window

DESIGN SIZE   4 x 2¾in (10 x 7cm)

PERSONALIZE   Stitch the appropriate age, making sure the rope aligns properly.

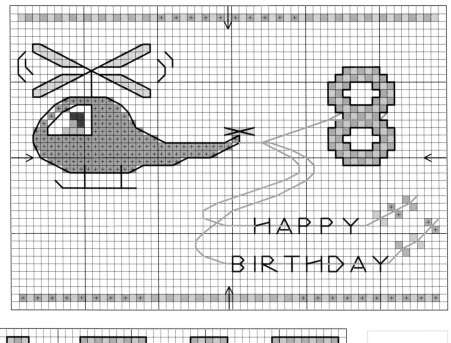

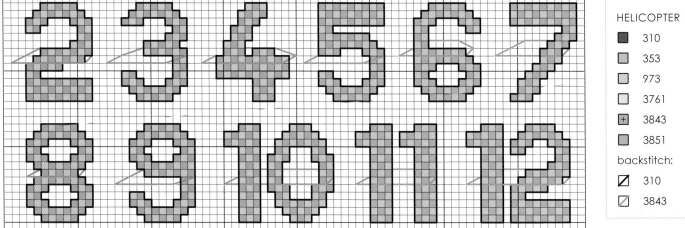

HELICOPTER	
■	310
▨	353
▨	973
□	3761
+	3843
▨	3851

backstitch:

◩	310
◩	3843

Monster Birthday

Send a youngster some gruesome greetings!

* Yellow 14-count Aida, 5 x 5in (12.5 x 12.5cm)
* DMC stranded cottons (floss) as listed in the key
* Purple double-fold card with a 4in (10cm) square window

DESIGN SIZE   3¹⁄₈ x 3¹⁄₈in (8 x 8cm).

PERSONALIZE   Stitch the appropriate age.

TO MOUNT   Add a double mount in a contrasting colour.

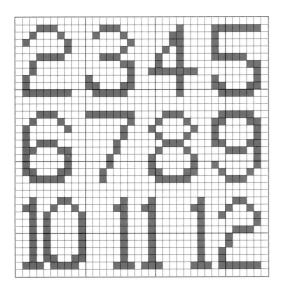

MONSTER BIRTHDAY			
■	310	▨	907
◉	350	⊞	blanc
⊠	550	backstitch:	
■	553	⊘	310
■	606	⊘	550
⊡	745	⊘	606

Ballerina Bunny

Make someone's birthday tu-tu marvellous.

* White 28-count evenweave, 6½ x 5in (16 x 12cm)
* DMC stranded cottons (floss) as listed in the key
* Lilac double-fold card with a 4½ x 2⅞in (11 x 7cm) rectangular window

DESIGN SIZE 4 x 2¾in (10 x 6.5cm)

PERSONALIZE Substitute the appropriate age by joining the ribbon at the marked position.

BALLERINA BUNNY		
⊙ 151	backstitch:	
▨ 209	◪ 209	
▨ 352	◪ 317	
⊞ 604	◪ 352	
▨ 3856	french knots:	
	⊠ 317	

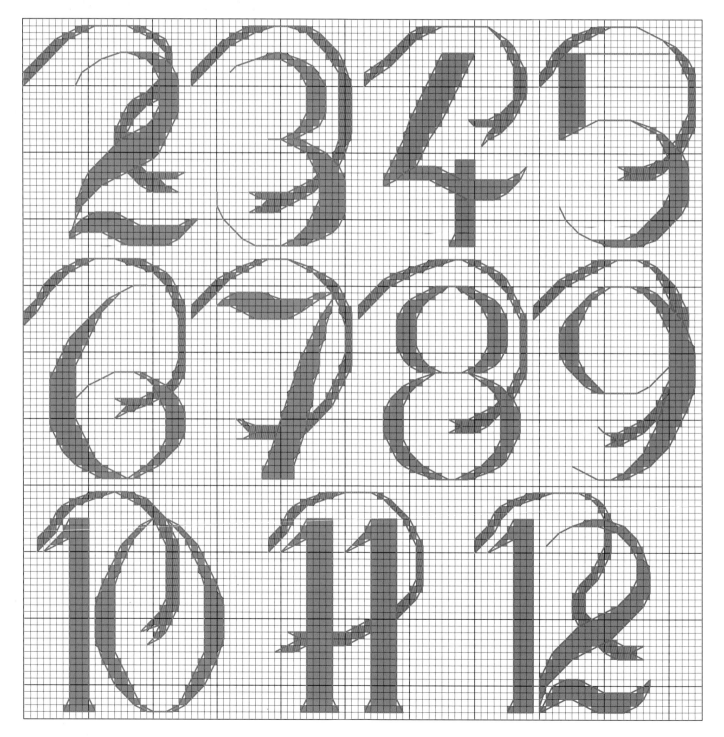

BALLERINA BUNNY

⊙	151	backstitch:	
▨	209	◪	209
▨	352	◪	317
+	604	◪	352
▨	3856	french knots:	
		⊠	317

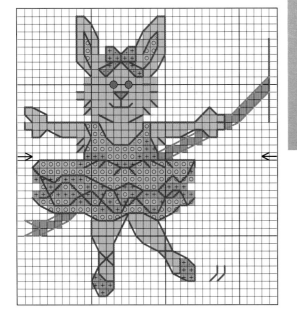

Rainbow Days

Most girls will love this burst of bright wishes.

* White 14-count Aida, 4 x 4in (10 x 10cm)
* DMC stranded cottons (floss) as listed in the key
* Salmon double-fold card with a 2¾ x 2¾in (7 x 7cm) square window

DESIGN SIZE 2½ x 2½in (6.5 x 6.5cm)

NOTES Refer to the chart on page 43 to work the appropriate age. Add a bow of ribbon in two colours.

GIFT IDEA See page 46 for a matching gift.

RAINBOW DAYS

▢	307
▨	554
▨	809
▢	954
▨	3708
backstitch:	
◪	553

MEMORABLE MOMENTS

The excitement doesn't end when childhood does. Life is packed with moments when a little support or applause will be most welcome. Here are designs to match all of those occasions: big, small and in-between.

ACHIEVEMENTS

ENGAGEMENT

WEDDING

WEDDING ANNIVERSARY

A FRESH START

NEW HORIZONS

FRIENDSHIP

SADDER MOMENTS

WITH THANKS

GIFT IDEAS

Congratulations Tag

Stitch the tag design on a 4 x 3in (10 x 7.5cm) piece of white 16-count Aida. Mount it in a red double-fold card with a 2¼ x 1¼in (6 x 3cm) window.

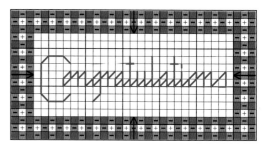

GRADUATION

				french knots:	
■	535	⊞	blanc	■	666
■	666	backstitch:		⊠	3799
⊠	3326	⁄	666		
▨	3364	⁄	3799		
▨	3713				

TAG

■	349
–	352
⊞	blanc
backstitch:	
⁄	817

Graduation

Go the whole hog for someone who has gained a certificate or degree.

* Taupe 28-count evenweave, 4 x 5in (10 x 12cm)
* DMC stranded cottons (floss) as listed in the key
* Red double-fold card with a 3⅛ x 4in (8 x 10cm) oval window

DESIGN SIZE   2¼ x 3¾in (5.5 x 9cm)

TO FINISH   Mount the stitched work in the card and decorate the front with gold stars.

Top Dog

Has someone done something to bark about?

* Cream 14-count Aida, 4 x 5in (10 x 12.5cm)
* DMC stranded cottons (floss) as listed in the key
* Cobalt double-fold card with a 3 x 4in (8 x 10cm) oval window

DESIGN SIZE   1¾ x 3in (4.7 x 7.8cm)

GIFT IDEA   See page 68 for a fun gift idea.

TOP DOG			
■	310		backstitch:
▨	606	⧄	310
▨	726	⧄	606
+	972		french knots:
▨	996	●	310
⊙	3843		

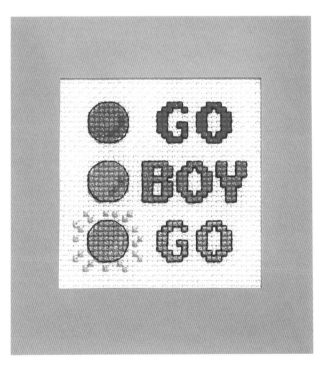

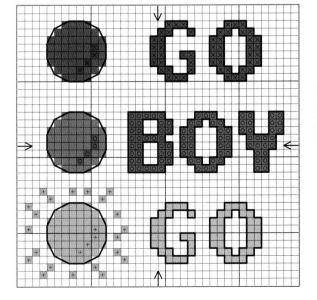

DRIVING TEST	
✕	349
▨	351
▨	704
⊙	721
▨	722
+	3348
backstitch:	
⧄	310

Driving Test

Give a new driver the green light!

* White 14-count Aida, 4 x 4in (10 x 10cm)
* DMC stranded cottons (floss) as listed in the key
* Lime green double-fold card with a 3 x 3in (7.6 x 7.6cm) square window

DESIGN SIZE   2½ x 2½in (6.5 x 6.5cm)

PERSONALIZE   For a female, stitch the word 'GIRL' to replace 'BOY', using the alphabet on page 101.

Engagement

Send your congratulations with this pretty design.

* White 14-count Aida, 4 x 6in (10 x 15cm)
* DMC stranded cottons (floss) as listed in the key
* Blue parchment double-fold card with a 2⁷⁄₈ x 4³⁄₈in (7 x 11cm) rectangular window

DESIGN SIZE 2³⁄₄ x 3⁵⁄₈in (7 x 9cm)

TO MOUNT Cut strips of blue card and stick them to the inside of the card blank to frame the top and bottom of the design.

ENGAGEMENT

▨	726	backstitch:
■	912	◪ 3845
◉	3761	
▨	3846	
＋	blanc	

Lovebirds

This dove duo would suit an engagement, a marriage, or even an anniversary.

* Peach 14-count Aida, 4 x 4in (10 x 10cm)
* DMC stranded cottons (floss) as listed in the key
* Peach parchment double-fold card with a 3¼in (8.3cm) round window

DESIGN SIZE 2⁵⁄₈ x 2⁵⁄₈in (6.5 x 6.5cm)

Wedding Sampler

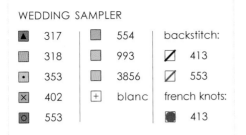

WEDDING SAMPLER

▲	317	▨	554	backstitch:	
▨	318	▨	993	◨	413
▪	353	▨	3856	◨	553
✕	402	⊞	blanc	french knots:	
◎	553			◼	413

Personalize this with names of the bride and groom, using the alphabet on page 100.

* White 28-count evenweave, 5 x 5in (13 x 13cm)
* DMC stranded cottons (floss) as listed in the key
* Lilac double-fold card with a 4in (10cm) square window

DESIGN SIZE 3½ x 3½in (9 x 9cm)

TAG Stitch the hat and names on 4 x 3in (10 x 7.5cm) white 28-count evenweave. Mount in a tag with a 2¼ x 1¼in (5.7 x 3cm) rectangular opening. Alternatively, stitch tags with a single name and use as place settings for the bridal party.

LOVEBIRDS

▨	352	▨	3348
✕	451	⊞	3865
▨	453	backstitch:	
▨	742	◨	451
▨	977		

10th Anniversary

Break open the champagne!

* White 14-count Aida, 4 x 4in (10 x 10cm)
* DMC stranded cottons (floss) as listed in the key
* Lavender double-fold card with a 2¼ x 2¾in (5.6 x 7.1cm) rectangular window

DESIGN SIZE 2 x 2⅝in (5 x 6.5cm)

TO FINISH Glue some sequins onto the card mount for added sparkle.

10th ANNIVERSARY	
◎	156
▨	209
▢	677
▨	726
▨	3747
backstitch:	
◪	160
◪	208

20th Anniversary

China symbolizes twenty happy years.

* Yellow 14-count Aida, 4 x 4in (10 x 10cm)
* DMC stranded cottons (floss) as listed in the key
* Cream double-fold card with a 2¼ x 2¾in (5.6 x 7.1cm) rectangular opening

DESIGN SIZE 2 x 2⅝in (5 x 6.5cm)

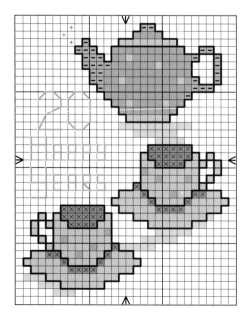

20th ANNIVERSARY	
☒	209
▨	211
▨	809
▬	913
▢	955
+	blanc
backstitch:	
◪	911
◪	3799

Twined Roses

This romantic design can be adapted for a silver, ruby or gold wedding anniversary.

* White 14-count Aida, 5 x 6in (12.5 x 15cm)
* DMC stranded cottons (floss) as listed in the key
* Silver/ruby/gold double-fold card with a 3½ x 5¼in (8.9 x 13.3cm) rectangular window

DESIGN SIZE 3 x 4⅛in (7.3 x 10.3cm)

PERSONALIZE Use numbers on page 100 for specific dates.

A sample of the ruby colour scheme is on page 48.

TWINED ROSES		SILVER 25 years	RUBY 40 years	GOLD 50 years
■ 400	⊙	5283	321	3820
■ 437	⊟	415	350	726
☒ 701	⊞	762	352	727
☐ 703	backstitch:			
⊙ 3776	⟋	5283	321	3820
	⟋	400	400	400
	⟋	699	699	699

New Job

Point the way to job satisfaction!

* White 14-count Aida, 4 x 4in (10 x 10cm)
* DMC stranded cottons (floss) as listed in the key
* Blue double-fold card with a 3in (7.6cm) square window

DESIGN SIZE   2¾ x 2¾in (7 x 7cm)

NEW JOB	
☐	157
☐	165
⊠	435
☐	437
⊙	3838
⊞	3839
backstitch:	
⟋	310
⟋	435

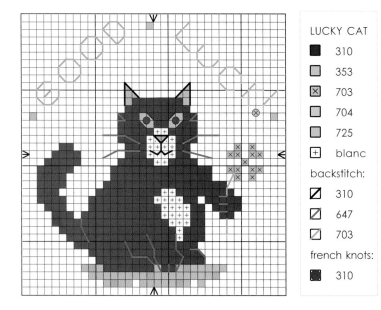

LUCKY CAT	
■	310
☐	353
⊠	703
☐	704
☐	725
⊞	blanc
backstitch:	
⟋	310
⟋	647
⟋	703
french knots:	
⬛	310

Lucky Cat

Stitch this for anyone taking a big step in life.

* Yellow 14-count Aida, 4 x 4in (10 x 10cm)
* DMC stranded cottons (floss) as listed in the key
* Sunflower double-fold card with a 3¼in (8.3cm) round window

DESIGN SIZE   2½ x 2½in (6.3 x 6.3cm)

Sweet Home

Every dog deserves a good home.

* Cream 24-count evenweave, 4 x 4in
  (10 x 10cm)
* DMC stranded cottons (floss) as listed
  in the key
* Red double-fold card with a 3in
  (7.6cm) square window

DESIGN SIZE 3 x 3in (7.5 x 7.5cm)

TO FINISH Draw gold paw prints on the mount.

SWEET HOME			
■ 350		⊠ 3776	
⊞ 743		▨ 3827	
□ 745		backstitch:	
■ 839		▨ 350	
▨ 3348		▨ 839	

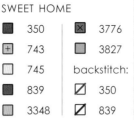

WELCOME	
▨	471
■	722
⊠	743
□	745
■	817
backstitch:	
▨	817
▨	898

Welcome

Send a warm welcome with this design.

* Sand 14-count Aida, 4 x 5in (10 x 12.5cm)
* DMC stranded cottons (floss) as listed in the key
* Ivory double-fold card with a 2¾ x 3½in
  (7 x 9cm) rectangular window

DESIGN SIZE 2½ x 3¼in (6.3 x 8cm)

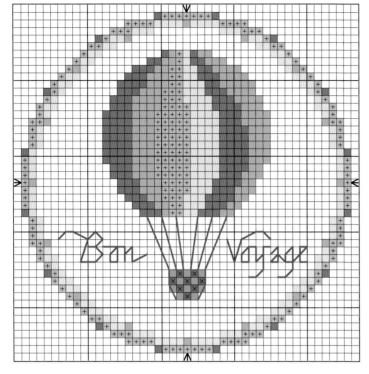

BON VOYAGE

▨	351	▨	3348
⊠	435	backstitch:	
▨	437	◪	435
⊞	743	◪	470
☐	745		

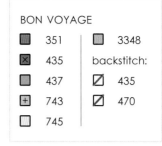

Bon Voyage

Bid a traveller a fond farewell with this motif.

* Cream 14-count Aida, 4½ x 4½in (12 x 12cm)
* DMC stranded cottons (floss) as listed in the key
* Ivory double-fold card with a 3½in (9cm) round window

DESIGN SIZE   3¼ x 3¼in (8 x 8cm)

GIFT IDEA   See page 69 for a gift idea featuring this design.

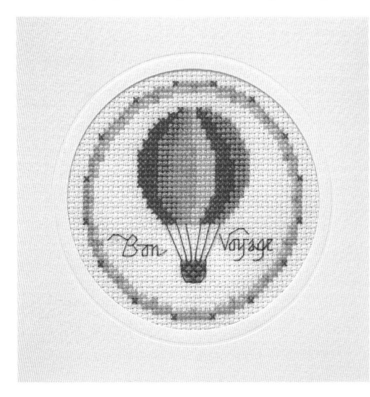

Welcome Home

It can be quite strange coming home after a long trip!

* Blue 25-count evenweave, 4 x 5in (10 x 12.5cm)
* DMC stranded cottons (floss) as listed in the key
* Lavender double-fold card with a 3 x 4½in (7.2 x 11cm) rectangular window

DESIGN SIZE   2⅝ x 3⅝in (6.6 x 9.2cm)

RETIREMENT

■	535	▨	3840
⊞	726	▨	3853
▨	728	backstitch:	
▨	798	◩	535
⊙	799	◩	798

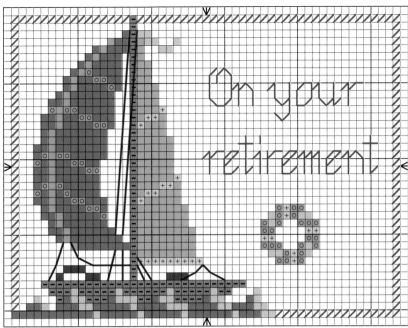

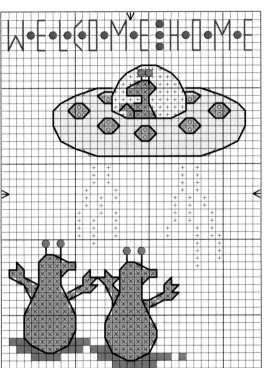

Retirement

Send a friend or colleague sailing off on a happy retirement.

* White 14-count Aida, 5 x 4in (12.5 x 10cm)
* DMC stranded cottons (floss) as listed in the key
* Cobalt double-fold card with a 4 x 3in (10 x 7.5cm) rectangular window

DESIGN SIZE 3¾ x 2⁷/₈in (9.5 x 7cm)

TO STITCH Use two strands for diagonal stitches around the border.

WELCOME HOME

⊙	444
☐	445
▨	905
⊠	907
⊞	white
backstitch:	
◩	310
◩	3837
french knots:	
◼	905
◼	3837

Best Friends

At nap time, only the best of friends share a pillow.

* Peach 28-count evenweave, 6 x 4½in (15 x 12cm)
* DMC stranded cottons (floss) as listed in the key
* Peach double-fold card with a 4 x 3¼in (10 x 8cm) oval window

DESIGN SIZE   3½ x 2⅜in (8.8 x 6cm)

BEST FRIENDS			
▨	352	▢	3855
◼	535	⊞	blanc
▨	646	backstitch:	
▨	648	▨	535
◪	745	french knots:	
▬	3853	◼	535
◙	3854		

FRIENDSHIP			
▢	350	backstitch:	
▢	353	▨	817
▢	721	french knots:	
▢	725	◙	817
◙	817	◼	920
⊞	920		

RAINY DAY FRIEND

▨	722	⊠	3838	backstitch:		
✳	792	▨	3839	▨	911	
⊙	911	▦	3863	▨	928	
▨	913	▨	3864	▨	3799	
▨	928	⊞	blanc	french knots:		
■	3799			⊞	blanc	

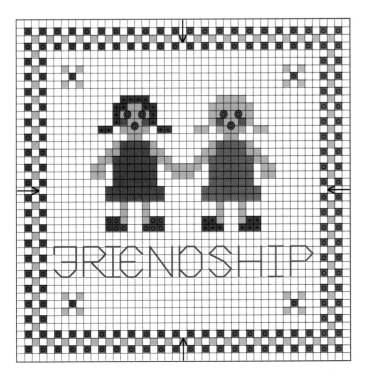

Rainy Day Friend

Here's a card for that special friend who sticks by you, no matter what the weather!

* Off-white 28-count evenweave, 4 x 4in (10 x 10cm)
* DMC stranded cottons (floss) as listed in the key
* Sky double-fold card with a 3in (7.6cm) square window

DESIGN SIZE 2¾ x 2¾in (7 x 7cm)

Friendship

Celebrate the bonds of friendship with this simple design.

* Sand 14-count Aida, 5 x 5in (12 x 12cm)
* DMC stranded cottons (floss) as listed in the key
* Pale green single-fold card at least 4 x 4in (10 x 10cm)

DESIGN SIZE 3 x 3in (7.5 x 7.5cm)

TO MOUNT After stitching, trim to five Aida blocks around the design. Fray two blocks and then stick on to the front of the card.

TO FINISH Glue a button on at each corner.

GIFT IDEA See page 68 for a gift idea based on this design.

Thinking of You Tag

Stitch the tag design on a 2½ x 2½in (6 x 6cm) piece of white 16-count Aida. Mount it in a sky double-fold card with a 1⅝in (4cm) square window or trim and stick it on a tag-shaped card.

TAG	
☐	725
☐	807
+	959
☐	3712
backstitch:	
◺	807

Get Well Soon

Here's a lovely view for someone who is unwell.

* White 14-count Aida, 4 x 5in (10 x 12cm)
* DMC stranded cottons (floss) as listed in the key
* Pale green double-fold card with a 3 x 3¾in (7.2 x 9.5cm) rectangular window

DESIGN SIZE   2¾ x 3½in (7 x 9cm)

GET WELL SOON					
☒	209	⊟	760	◉	3840
☐	211	☐	761	☐	3841
⊟	726	☐	772	⊡	3865
☐	727	☐	989	backstitch:	
◺	738	S	3328	◺	535
☐	739	+	3348	◺	3328

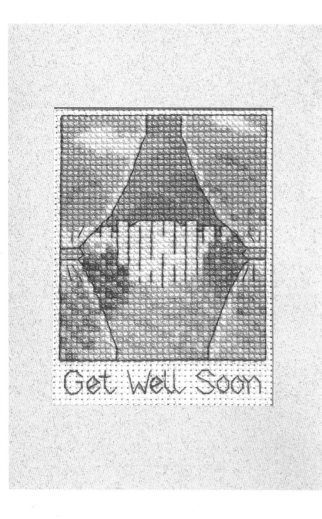

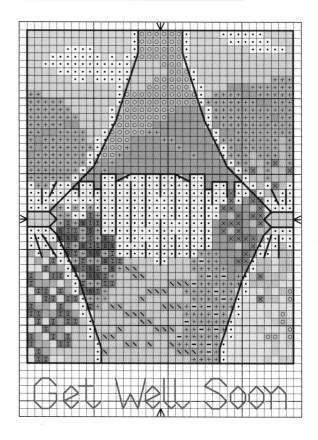

On Your Loss

In the language of flowers, lily-of-the-valley signifies the return of happiness, a fitting sentiment for a sympathy card.

* Grey-green 28-count evenweave, 4 x 4in (10 x 10cm)
* DMC stranded cottons (floss) as listed in the key
* Soft green double-fold card with a 3in (7.6cm) square window

DESIGN SIZE   2¾ x 2¾in (7 x 7cm)

MISSING YOU			
⊙	353	⊞	blanc
■	436		backstitch:
▨	581	◪	581
■	3799	◪	3799
☐	3822		french knots:
⊟	ecru	⊕	blanc

ON YOUR LOSS		
▨	906	
⊙	907	
⊞	blanc	
backstitch:		
◪	905	

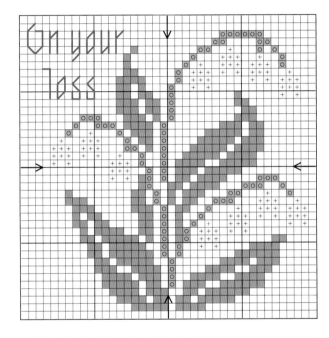

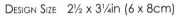

Missing You

These hopeful meerkats are on the lookout!

* Cream 28-count evenweave, 4 x 5in (10 x 12.5cm)
* DMC stranded cottons (floss) as listed in the key
* Dark cream double-fold card with a 2¾ x 3¾in (6.6 x 9.4cm) rectangular window

DESIGN SIZE   2½ x 3¼in (6 x 8cm)

Thank You

This card is as pretty as a posy of flowers and will last much longer.

* White 14-count Aida, 5 x 5in (12.5 x 12.5cm)
* DMC stranded cottons (floss) as listed in the key
* Lilac double-fold card with a 4in (10 cm) square window

DESIGN SIZE   3¾ x 3¾in (9.5 x 9.5cm)

TO STITCH   Use two strands of stranded cotton (floss) for the backstitch.

THANK YOU		
⊞ 210	⊠ 3608	
▨ 211	⊙ 3609	
▨ 340	backstitch:	
▢ 745	◿ 3609	
▨ 955		

MANY THANKS

▨	608	**backstitch:**	
☐	928	◪	608
◉	3340	◪	928
⊟	3341	◪	3799
☐	3716	◪	3819
■	3799	◪	3865
☐	3819	**french knots:**	
⊞	3865	■	3799

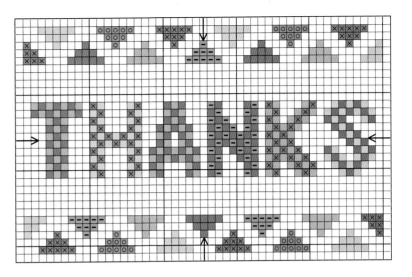

Many Thanks

Well-mannered pandas always show their gratitude with flowers!

* Peach 28-count evenweave, 4 x 5in (10 x 12cm)
* DMC stranded cottons (floss) as listed in the key
* Salmon double-fold card with a 2¾ x 4¼in (7.2 x 11cm) rectangular window

DESIGN SIZE 2⅜ x 3⅜in (6 x 8.4cm)

THANKS

▨	351	⊟	742
◉	722	☒	3340
☐	726	☐	3919

Thanks

Here's a bright and cheery way to say thank you.

* Cream 14-count Aida, 5 x 4in (12 x 10cm)
* DMC stranded cottons (floss) as listed in the key
* Bright yellow double-fold card with a 3¾ x 2¾in (9.4 x 6.6cm) rectangular window

DESIGN SIZE 3½ x 2¼in (8.8 x 5.4cm)

GIFT IDEA See page 69 for a gift idea based on this design.

Key Ring

Make a friend smile with this zippy keyring.

* Cream 14-count Aida, 3 x 4½in (7.5 x 11.2cm)
* DMC stranded cottons (floss) as listed in the key
* A metal keyring
* Ribbon

1 Cut the Aida fabric in two 2¼ x 3in (5.6 x 7.5cm) pieces. In the centre of one piece, stitch the Top Dog motif (excluding the podium), following the chart and key on page 51.

2 Lay the two pieces together, wrong sides facing. Cut a 4in (10cm) length of ribbon, slip it through the metal ring and tuck the ribbon ends between the Aida pieces. Pin to hold in place.

3 Secure the edges with large stitches using blue stranded cotton (floss).

Keepsake Box

Decorate a box for a friend to store cards or photographs.

* Sand 14-count Aida, 5 x 5in (12 x 12cm)
* DMC stranded cottons (floss) as listed in the key
* A cardboard box with lid
* Card to fit inside the box lid; ribbon

1 Stitch the Friendship motif on the Aida fabric, following the chart on page 63 and its key on page 62.

2 Mark a 3⅜in (8.5cm) square in the centre of the box lid and cut with a sharp knife to create an aperture.

3 Lay double-sided tape on the inside of the lid and stick the stitching in place. Use more tape to secure the piece of card in the box lid as a backing.

4 Cut a 6in (15cm) length of ribbon and secure it on one corner of the lid with double-sided tape. Repeat on the opposite corner, then add a ribbon bow.

Ring Pillow

Present this to a pair of nearly-weds.

* Peach 28-count evenweave, 5 x 10in (12 x 24cm)
* DMC stranded cottons (floss) as listed in the key
* Polyester stuffing
* Narrow ribbon

1 Cut the fabric in half. On one piece, stitch the Bells and Hearts design following the chart and key on page 55.

2 Place the two fabric squares together with right sides facing and sew a ½in (1cm) seam, leaving a gap for turning.

3 Turn the work right side out and fill with polyester stuffing. Neatly handsew the opening closed. Tie small ribbon bows and sew one on at each corner.

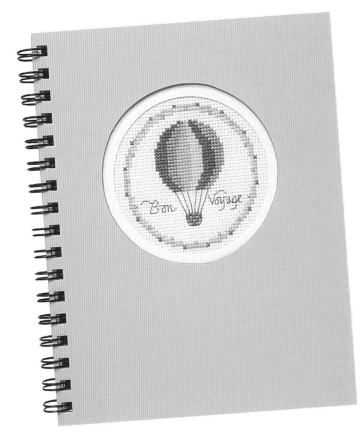

Travel Diary

Send a friend off on their travels with a lovely journal. You could also use this technique to mount another design and make a recipe book or general diary.

* Cream 14-count Aida, 5 x 5in (12 x 12cm)
* DMC stranded cottons (floss) as listed in the key
* A notebook with a stiff board cover
* Ivory double-fold card with a 3½in (9cm) round window
* A sheet of acetate (optional)

1 Stitch the Bon Voyage balloon design following the chart and key on page 60.

2 Mount the stitched Aida in the double-fold card. Note: if you wish to protect the cross stitching, you could fix a piece of acetate between the window section and the Aida.

3 Remove the back flap of the card.

4 Use compasses (or an upturned glass) to mark a circle with a radius of 2in (5cm) in pencil on the front cover of the notebook. With a sharp craft knife, cut carefully around the penci line and remove the circle (taking care not to cut the pages of the book).

5 Use double-sided tape to mount the framed card in the window, ensuring that it is centred.

Photo Frame

A photo portrait framed with a bright border makes a very personal gift for a friend.

* Cream 14-count Aida, 5 x 5in (12.5 x 12.5cm)
* DMC stranded cottons (floss) as listed in the key
* Two pieces of stiff card, each 4 x 4in (10 x 10cm)

1 Using the chart and key on page 67, stitch the top double row of triangles, so that the stitching begins ¾in (1.8cm) from the top of the fabric. Turn the book 90 degrees clockwise and stitch the same section again. Repeat this twice to form a box border.

2 Mark a 2in (5cm) square in the centre of one card section and carefully cut it out with a sharp knife. Mark a 1in (3cm) square in the centre of the Aida fabric and remove it.

3 Attach the fabric onto the cardboard frame with double-sided tape. Snip darts in the fabric so that you can fold and secure the overlapping edges onto the back of the frame. Dab some PVA (white) glue inside the corners to prevent fraying.

4 Position and tape a photo in the frame. Stick the second piece of card on as a backing for the frame.

BIRTHDAY CELEBRATIONS

Birthdays are the chance we get to remind friends and family that they mean a great deal to us. Think about that person and stitch a card that is perfect for him or her.

HAPPY BIRTHDAY

TEEN BIRTHDAYS

MEN'S BIRTHDAYS

MEN FOLK

WOMEN'S BIRTHDAYS

FEMALE FAMILY

STAR SIGNS

HOBBIES & INTERESTS

SPORTS & LEISURE

SPECIAL BIRTHDAYS

GIFT IDEAS

Tulip Tag

Stitch the tag design on a 2½in (5cm) square of white 14-count Aida. Trim and stick it on a tag-shaped card.

TULIP TAG	
◎	3340
▨	3341
☒	3347
▨	3348
backstitch:	
▨	355

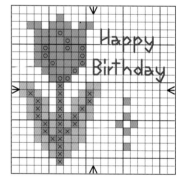

Birthday Bear

Birthdays deserve a really big fuss.

* Yellow 28-count evenweave, 5 x 6in (12 x 15cm)
* DMC stranded cottons (floss) as listed in the key
* Sunflower double-fold card with a 3 x 4in (8 x 10cm) oval window

DESIGN SIZE   2½ x 3⅜in (6 x 8.4cm)

TO FINISH   Stick on some stars for extra finesse.

BIRTHDAY BEAR			
◁	726	▨	3854
☐	727	backstitch:	
☒	911	▨	310
▨	913	▨	911
▨	3022	french knots:	
◎	3853	◾	310

Oops!

Missed a birthday? Quick, beaver away on this design and send belated greetings.

* Coffee 28-count evenweave, 5 x 5in (12 x 12cm)
* DMC stranded cottons (floss) as listed in the key
* Ivory double-fold card with a 3⅜in (8.3cm) round window

DESIGN SIZE   2⅝ x 2⅝in (6.6 x 6.6cm)

SAMPLER	
▨	165
◩	166
⊙	553
▨	554
☒	603
▨	605

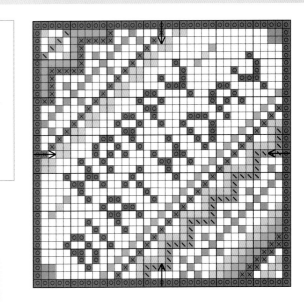

OOPS!	
▨	166
■	310
▨	422
☒	435
⊙	3826
⊟	3827
⊞	blanc
backstitch:	
▱	310
▱	905
french knots:	
◼	310

Birthday Sampler

Give this jaunty card to someone you love.

* White 14-count Aida, 3½ x 3½in (9 x 9cm)
* DMC stranded cottons (floss) as listed in the key
* Lilac double-fold card with a 2⅝in (7cm) square window

DESIGN SIZE   2½ x 2½in (6.5 x 6.5cm)

TO FINISH   Cut paper hearts and stick them on.

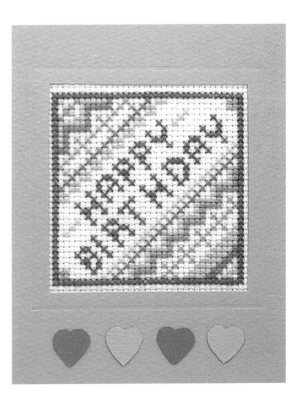

SWINGING SISTER

- 553
- 704
- 722
- 726
- 3770

backstitch:
- 310
- 3801

french knots:
- 310
- 3801

Groovy Guys

Two hip designs for teens or your siblings!

* Yellow 14-count Aida, 4 x 5in (10 x 12.5cm)
* DMC stranded cottons (floss) as listed in the key
* A double-fold card with a 3 x 4in (8 x 10cm) oval window

DESIGN SIZE   2¾ x 3½in (7 x 9cm)

SOUL BROTHER		
704	3770	553
722	3801	french knots:
726	backstitch:	310
799	310	553

Cool Cat

Here's one for the man with attitude.

* Blue-grey 28-count evenweave, 5 x 5in (12 x 12cm)
* DMC stranded cottons (floss) as listed
* Sky double-fold card with a 3½in (9cm) round window

DESIGN SIZE   3 x 3⅛in (7.3 x 7.6cm)

GIFT IDEA   See page 93 for a matching gift.

COOL CAT	
■	310
■	996
⊙	3827
■	3854
+	blanc
backstitch:	
◪	310
◪	721

Hoppy Birthday

Here's a bright and bouncy card.

* Teal 28-count evenweave, 4 x 4½in (11 x 12cm)
* DMC stranded cottons (floss) as listed in key
* Turquoise double-fold card with a 3¼ x 3¾in (8.5 x 9.5cm) rectangular window

DESIGN SIZE   3 x 3½in (7.7 x 8.7cm)

HOPPY DAY	
▢	822
⊙	976
▨	977
⊠	3826
backstitch:	
◪	310
◪	3814
◪	3816

Handy Man

There must be one man in your family who knows a whatsit from a thingummy!

* White 28-count evenweave, 4 x 6in (10 x 15cm)
* DMC stranded cottons (floss) as listed in the key
* Ruby double-fold card with a 2⅞ x 4½in (7 x 11cm) rectangular window

DESIGN SIZE   2½ x 4in (6.3 x 10cm)

PERSONALIZE   Select the appropriate kin from the chart below.

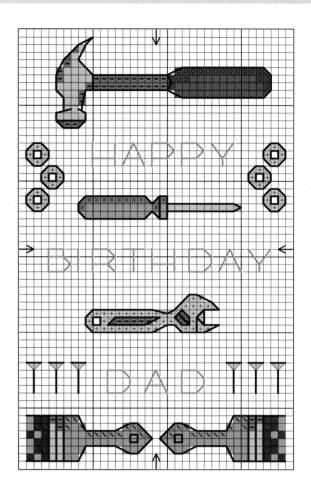

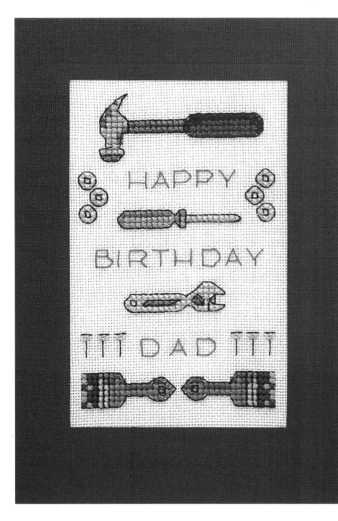

HANDY MAN			
■	350	▨	907
⊟	414	▨	958
☐	415	◪	3814
■	535	**backstitch:**	
⊞	775	◩	3799
◉	817	◪	3812
☒	906		

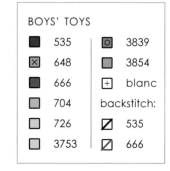

BOYS' TOYS			
■	535	◉	3839
☒	648	☐	3854
■	666	⊞	blanc
☐	704	**backstitch:**	
☐	726	◪	535
☐	3753	◪	666

Boys' Toys

No matter the age, they're always boys at heart.

* Off-white 28-count evenweave, 4 x 4in (10 x 10cm)
* DMC stranded cottons (floss) as listed in the key
* Cobalt double-fold card with a 2¾ x 2¼in (7 x 6cm) rectangular window

DESIGN SIZE   2½ x 2in (6.3 x 5cm)

PERSONALIZE   Select the appropriate kin from the chart on the left.

Shells

For the romantic soul (or the salty sea-dog).

* White 14-count Aida, 4 x 4in (10 x 10cm)
* DMC stranded cottons (floss) as listed in the key
* Sky double-fold card with a 3in (7.5cm) square window

DESIGN SIZE   2¾ x 2¾in (6.8 x 6.8cm).

PERSONALIZE   For other relatives, see the text charts on the left and on page 80.

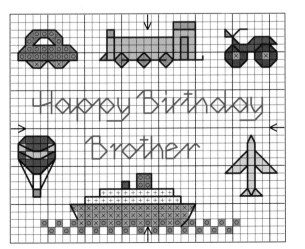

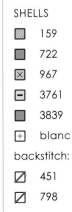

SHELLS	
▨	159
■	722
☒	967
⊟	3761
▨	3839
⊞	blanc
backstitch:	
◹	451
◹	798

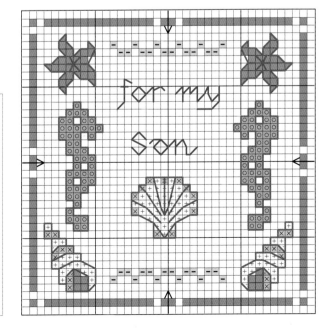

Butterfly Quartet

This pretty butterfly collection will brighten the day of someone special.

* White 14-count Aida, 5 x 5in (12.5 x 12.5cm)
* DMC stranded cottons (floss) as listed in the key
* Ivory double-fold card with a 4 x 4in (10 x 10cm) square window

DESIGN SIZE   3½ x 3½in (8.75 x 8.75cm)

GIFT IDEA   See page 92 for a gift decorated with this butterfly motif.

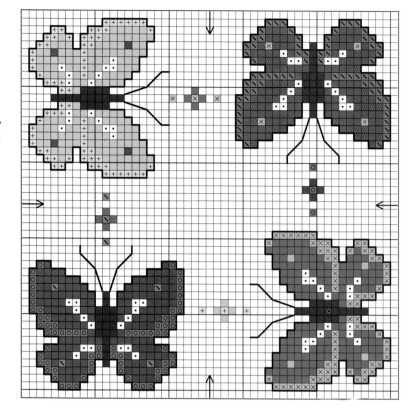

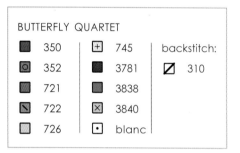

BUTTERFLY QUARTET				
■	350	⊞	745	backstitch:
◉	352	■	3781	⧄ 310
▨	721	▩	3838	
◪	722	⊠	3840	
▢	726	⊡	blanc	

Unicorn

Here's one for a truly fabulous birthday.

* Blue 14-count Aida, 4 x 6in (10 x 15cm)
* DMC stranded cottons (floss) as listed in the key
* Cobalt double-fold card with a 3 x 4⅜in (7.5 x 11cm) rectangular window

DESIGN SIZE   2¾ x 4in (7 x 10cm)

TO FINISH   Rule a silver line around the window.

UNICORN	
■	310
⊟	414
□	415
▨	798
⊞	blanc
backstitch:	
◨	413
◨	798

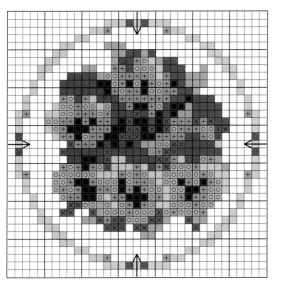

Pansy Circlet

Greet a birthday girl with this pretty bouquet.

* White 28-count evenweave, 4 x 4in (10 x 10cm)
* DMC stranded cottons (floss) as listed in the key
* Yellow double-fold card with a 2¾in (7cm) round window

DESIGN SIZE   2⅜ x 2⅜in (6 x 6cm)

GIFT IDEA   See page 93 for a matching gift.

PANSY CIRCLET	
▨	550
▨	552
⊙	725
□	726
☒	904
▨	907
⊞	972

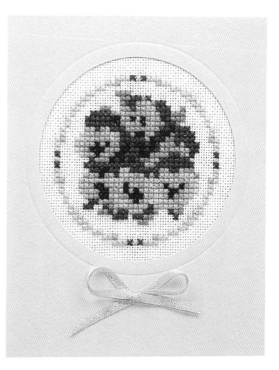

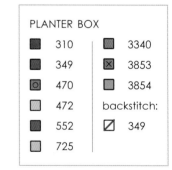

SWIMMING LESSON

☒	369	◙	3766
■	722	⊞	blanc
☐	744		backstitch:
■	989	◪	535
⊡	3753	◪	722
☐	3761		french knots:
		▦	535

Swimming Lesson

This scene would be ideal for either a mother or a daughter.

* Pale green 28-count evenweave, 5 x 4in (12 x 10cm)
* DMC stranded cottons (floss) as listed in the key
* Sky double-fold card with a 4 x 3in (10 x 8cm) oval window

DESIGN SIZE　3¾ x 2½in (9 x 6.5cm)

PLANTER BOX			
■	310	■	3340
■	349	☒	3853
◙	470	☐	3854
☐	472		backstitch:
■	552	◪	349
☐	725		

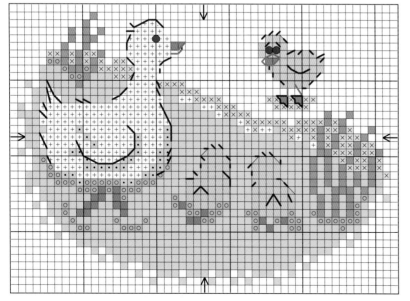

Superchef

For anyone who's a dab hand in the kitchen.

* White 28-count evenweave, 4 x 6in (10 x 15cm)
* DMC stranded cottons (floss) as listed in the key
* Ivory double-fold card with a 2⅞ x 4½in (7 x 11cm) rectangular window

DESIGN SIZE 2½ x 4in (6.3 x 10cm)

PERSONALIZE Select the appropriate kin from the text chart below.

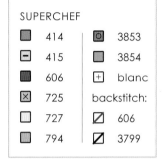

SUPERCHEF	
414	⊙ 3853
− 415	3854
606	+ blanc
⊠ 725	backstitch:
727	⧄ 606
794	⧄ 3799

Planter Box

Here's a floral card that will keep on blooming.

* White 14-count Aida, 4 x 3½in (10 x 9cm)
* DMC stranded cottons (floss) as listed in the key
* Pale green double-fold card with a 2¾ x 2¼in (7 x 5.5cm) rectangular window

DESIGN SIZE 2½ x 2in (6.5 x 5cm).

PERSONALIZE See the text chart on page 80 for other relatives.

Star Signs

These signs of the zodiac are quick to stitch and a charm to receive. You could make the whole series and have them handy for all your friends.

* Black 28-count evenweave, 3½ x 3½in (9 x 9cm)
* DMC stranded cottons (floss) as listed in the key
* Gold double-fold card with a 2⅝in (6.5cm) square window

DESIGN SIZE   2¼ x 2¼in (5.5 x 5.5cm)

GIFT IDEA   For a gift idea based on these designs, see page 93. The whole series would also look good stitched and framed.

STAR SIGNS	
▨	725
◎	744
backstitch:	
▧	744

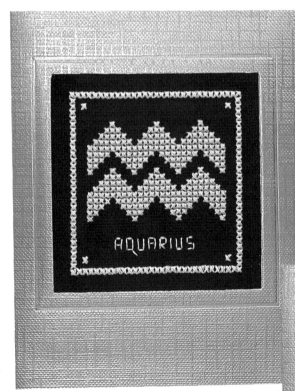

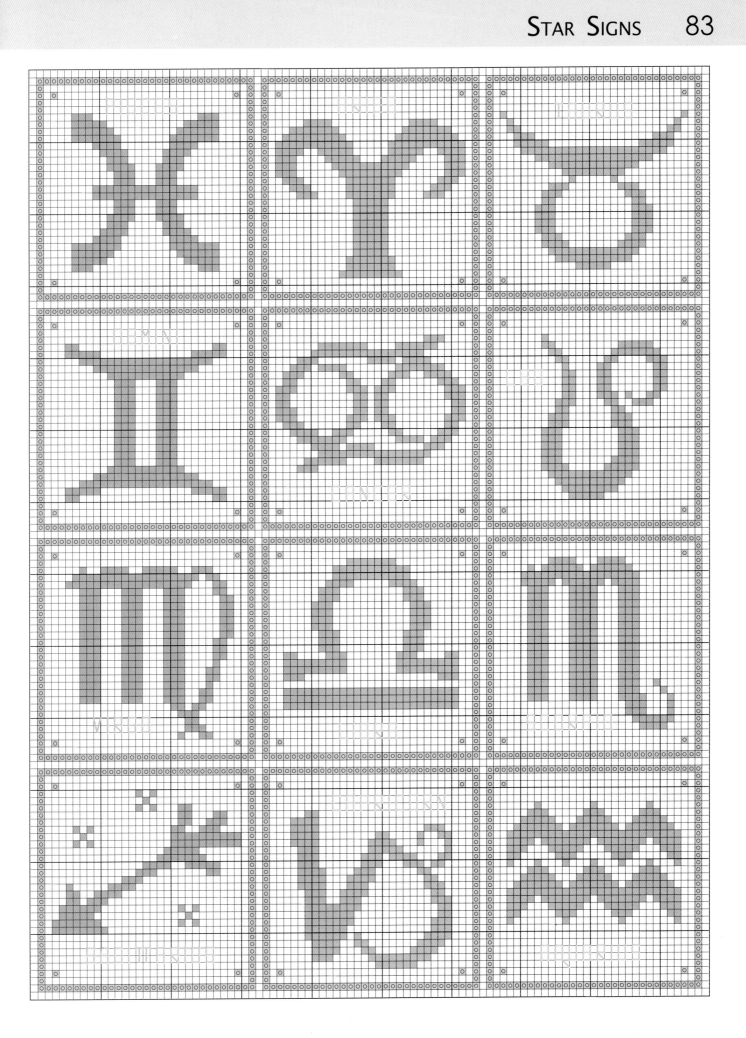

Pastimes

Everyone loves to receive a card that matches their personality. You could mix motifs from the following designs to make a very individual card.

* White 14-count Aida, 4 x 4in (10 x 10cm)
* DMC stranded cottons (floss) as listed in the key
* Coloured double-fold card with a 3in (7.5cm) square opening

DESIGN SIZE 2¾ x 2¾in (7 x 7cm)

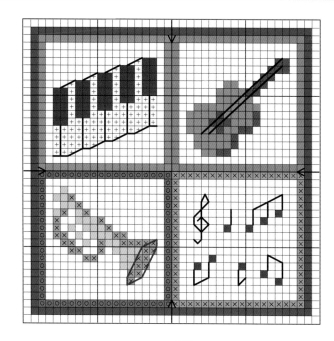

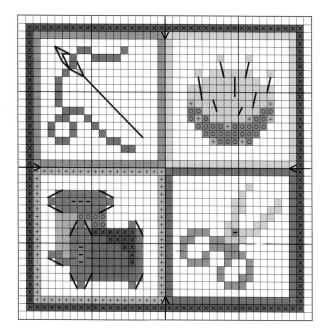

SEWING			
☐	157	☐	841
☐	165	☐	3341
☒	350	☐	3819
☐	351	☐	3839
☐	414	backstitch:	
☐	415	☑	413

MUSIC			
☐	310	☒	972
☐	434	☐	3608
☐	553	☐	blanc
☐	722	backstitch:	
☐	726	☑	310
☐	917	☑	434

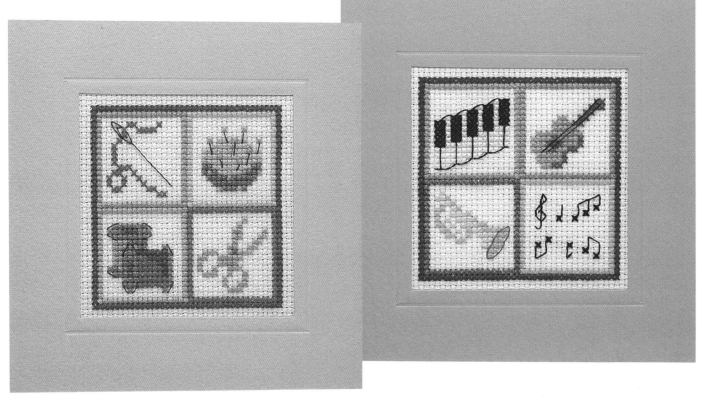

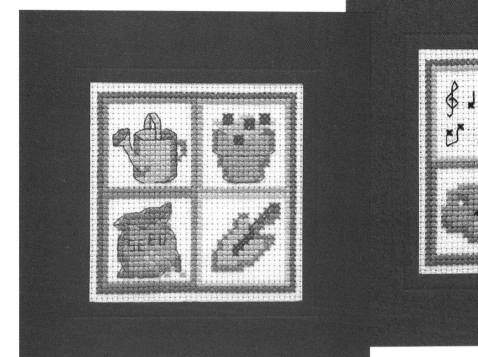

GARDENING

■	606	◎	3022	T	3826
+	954		3024	−	3849
◪	976	■	3787	**backstitch:**	
■	977	■	3814	╱	3787
⊠	989	▨	3819	╱	3826

ARTS

■	310	■	729
+	371		742
−	414	◎	782
	415	**backstitch:**	
■	471	╱	310
⊠	720	╱	414
	722		

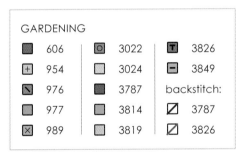

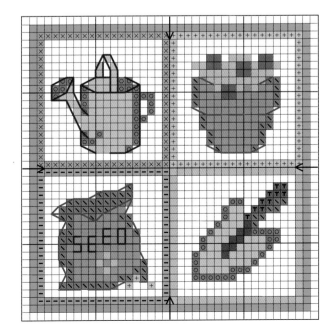

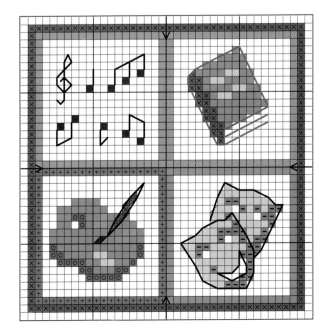

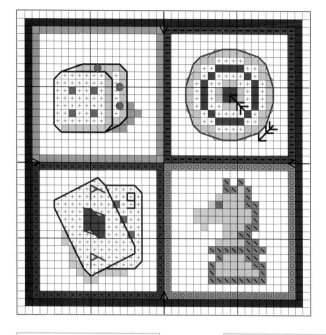

Activities

Choose a birthday card for a sporty type
from this array.

* White 14-count Aida, 4 x 4in (10 x 10cm)
* DMC stranded cottons (floss) as listed in the key
* Coloured double-fold card with a 3in (7.5cm)
  square opening

DESIGN SIZE   2¾ x 2¾in (7 x 7cm)

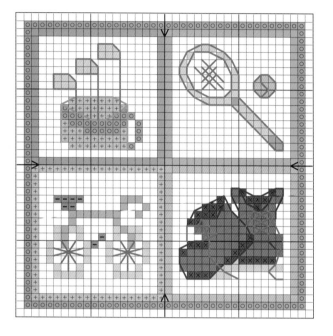

GAMES			
■	210	■	718
■	310	✖	3837
◩	414	➕	blanc
■	415		backstitch:
■	550	◪	310
◎	554	◪	666
■	666	◪	3837

SPORTS			
✖	301	◎	3812
▬	414	■	3819
■	415	■	3853
■	911		backstitch:
➕	959	◪	414
■	996	◪	3812

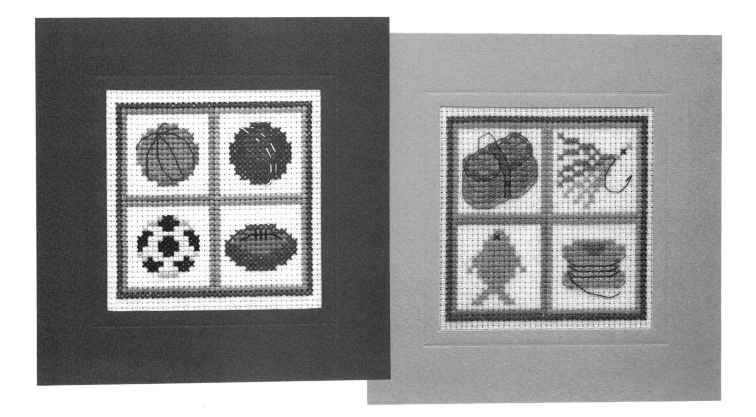

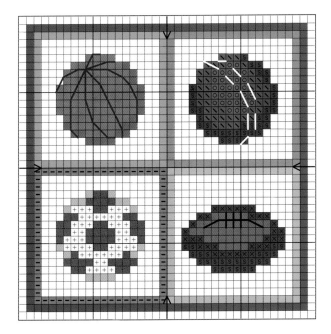

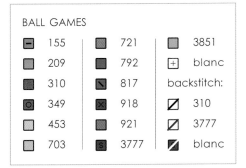

BALL GAMES

▬	155	▨	721	▢	3851	
▢	209	▨	792	⊞	blanc	
▨	310	◣	817	backstitch:		
◉	349	✕	918	◿	310	
▢	453	▨	921	◿	3777	
▢	703	▨	3777	◢	blanc	

FISHING

■	413	▨	799
⊞	435	▢	959
▨	437	◉	3846
▢	453	backstitch:	
▢	704	◿	413
✕	798	◿	435

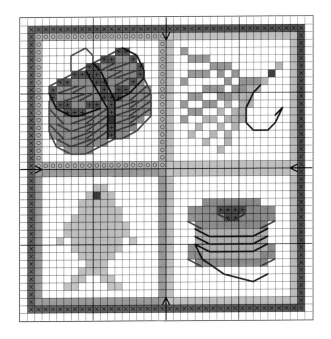

Keys

Give a young adult the keys to the kingdom!

* Black 28-count evenweave, 4 x 4in (10 x 10cm)
* DMC stranded cottons (floss) as listed in the key
* Silver double-fold card with a 3in (7.5cm) square window

DESIGN SIZE   2¾ x 2¾in (7 x 7cm)

NOTE   For '18', refer to the chart on the right.

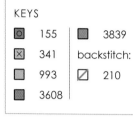

18TH			
☐	307	backstitch:	
✛	436	⊘	307
▨	437	⊘	310
■	666	⊘	400
◉	817	⊘	3843
▦	3843		

KEYS			
◉	155	▦	3839
✕	341	backstitch:	
▨	993	⊘	210
▦	3608		

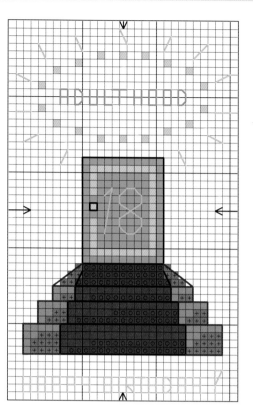

18th

The threshold of adulthood is a big step.

* Red 14-count Aida, 4 x 5in (10 x 12cm)
* DMC stranded cottons (floss) as listed in the key
* Double-fold card measuring 4 x 5½in (10 x 14cm)

DESIGN SIZE   2¼ x 3¾in (5.5 x 9cm)

TO MOUNT   Use the template on page 102 to cut the window.

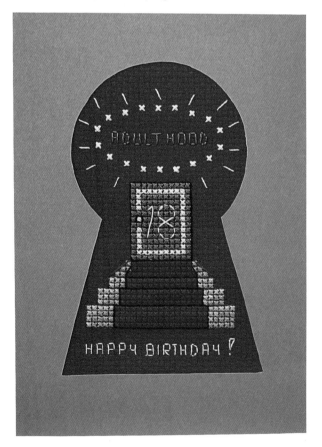

Life Begins

Forty years young and loving it!

* Blue 14-count Aida, 4 x 3½in (10 x 9cm)
* DMC stranded cottons (floss) as listed in the key
* Sky double-fold card with a 2¾ x 2¼in (7 x 5.5cm) rectangular window

DESIGN SIZE 2½ x 2in (6 x 5cm)

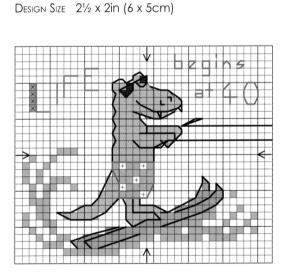

LIFE BEGINS	
▨	704
☒	995
▨	3608
■	3799
▨	3846
▨	3856
⊞	blanc
backstitch:	
◪	995
◪	3799

Hippos

Hippos really know how to celebrate.

* White 28-count evenweave, 4 x 6in (10 x 15cm)
* DMC stranded cottons (floss) as listed
* Peach double-fold card with a 3 x 4½in (7 x 11cm) rectangular window

DESIGN SIZE 2¾ x 4¼in (7 x 10.5cm)

PERSONALIZE Other numbers are charted on page 101.

HIPPOS	
▨	444
■	606
■	718
▨	741
backstitch:	
◪	310
◪	718
french knots:	
▪	310

Cake Overload

For someone suffering candle overload.

* White 28-count evenweave, 4 x 4in (10 x 10cm)
* DMC stranded cottons (floss) as listed
* Sunflower double-fold card with a 3in (7.5cm) square window

DESIGN SIZE   2¼ x 3¾in (5.5 x 9cm)

PERSONALIZE   You could substitute other numbers from the chart on page 100.

TO DECORATE   Draw gold swirls on the mount.

FRUIT TREE	
☒	720
☐	722
◉	976
☐	977
⊞	3012
☐	3013
☐	3819
backstitch:	
◩	720
◩	3826

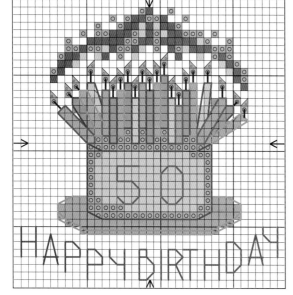

CAKE OVERLOAD			
☐	341	backstitch:	
☐	605	◩	340
⊞	703	◩	535
☐	740	◩	603
◉	743	◩	703
☐	744	◩	740
☐	3348		

Fruit Tree

A classic design for a landmark year.

* Cream 14-count Aida, 5 x 4in (12 x 10cm)
* DMC stranded cottons (floss) as listed in the key
* Tan double-fold card with a 4 x 3in (10 x 7.5cm) rectangular window

DESIGN SIZE   3 x 2½in (7 x 6.5cm)

PERSONALIZE   More ages appear on page 101.

TO MOUNT   Use a double mount to add style.

GIFT IDEA   See page 92 for a matching gift.

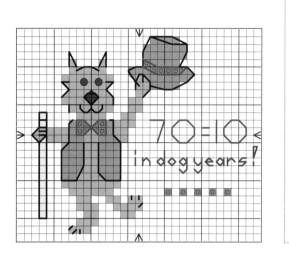

DOG YEARS	
▢	554
☐	762
◉	3608
◼	3799
▨	3856
backstitch:	
◻	553
◻	3607
◻	3799
french knots:	
◼	3799

Dog Years

Some acts deserve extra applause.

* Yellow 28-count evenweave, 4 x 3½in (10 x 9cm)
* DMC stranded cottons (floss) as listed
* Lilac double-fold card with a 2¾ x 2¼in (7 x 5.5cm) rectangular window

DESIGN SIZE   2¼ x 2in (5.5 x 4.6cm)

TO FINISH   Snip triangles pieces from the window frame, before mounting.

Good Wine

A card for the true connoisseur.

* Yellow 28-count evenweave, 4 x 6in (10 x 15cm)
* DMC stranded cottons (floss) as listed in the key
* Parchment double-fold card with a 2¾ x 4¼in (7.5 x 11cm) rectangular window

DESIGN SIZE   2¾ x 3½in (6.7 x 9cm)

TO MOUNT   Stick strips of contrasting card inside the window at the top and base.

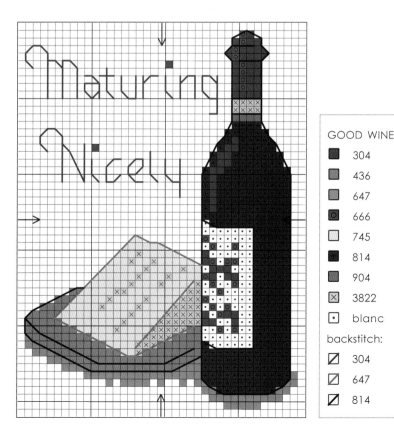

GOOD WINE	
◼	304
▩	436
▨	647
◉	666
▧	745
◼	814
▩	904
☒	3822
⊡	blanc
backstitch:	
◻	304
◻	647
◻	814

Fragrant Sachet

A citrus-scented sachet is a fresh idea for a present.

* Cream 14-count Aida, 5 x 12½in (12.5 x 32cm)
* DMC stranded cottons (floss) as listed in the key
* Polyester stuffing; citrus scent
* Lace trim; ribbon

1 Fold the Aida in half to form a 6¼ x 5in (16 x 12.5cm) rectangle. Following the chart and key on page 90, stitch the fruit tree design so that the baseline is ½in (1.5cm) from the folded base.

2 With the stitched design facing inwards, sew the side seams and zigzag all edges to prevent fraying. Fold over ½in (1cm) at the opening and press flat.

3 Pin a lace trim around the opening so that the decorative edge pokes out of the sachet. Stitch to secure the lace and the hem of the opening.

4 Shake a few drops of citrus scent onto some polyester stuffing and push it into the sachet. Tie the sachet closed with a ribbon.

Glasses Case

Everyone needs a case to protect that pair of glasses.

* Coloured 25-count evenweave, 8 x 9in (20 x 22.5cm)
* DMC stranded cottons (floss) as listed in the key
* Lining fabric
* Matching bias binding; a press stud (gripper snap)

1 Trace the glasses case pattern on page 102 onto paper and cut it out. Use this template to cut two pieces of Aida fabric: the backing section should be full sized; the front section should be trimmed along the dashed line.

2 Refer to the chart and key on page 78 to stitch a single butterfly on the front section, so that the design starts 2in (5cm) from the base of the fabric shape.

3 Cut two pieces of lining fabric to match the Aida pieces. Bind the top of the front layers with a strip of folded bias binding. Lay all the pieces together so that the stitching is on top and the lining pieces are inside.

4 Secure the sections together with long stitches around the raw edges. Bind the raw edges with a long strip of bias binding. Sew on a press stud (gripper snap) to secure the top flap.

Paperweight

Here's the ideal gift for a workaholic!

* Blue-grey 28-count evenweave, 6 x 6in (15 x 15cm)
* DMC stranded cottons (floss) as listed in the key
* Glass paperweight suitable for embroidery

1 Stitch the cat design, without the text, following the chart and key on page 75.

2 Centre the stitched fabric over the paper or card template supplied with the paperweight and trim to fit.

3 Mount the work in the paperweight according to the manufacturer's instructions.

Mirror Compact

Turn an old compact mirror into a small treasure.

* White 28-count evenweave, 4 x 4in (10 x 10cm)
* DMC stranded cottons (floss) as listed in the key
* Thin polyester wadding (batting)
* Stiff white cardboard
* A mirror from an old compact

1 Stitch the pansy design following the chart and key on page 79. Mark a 3½in (9cm) circle around the design and trim the fabric to this.

2 On stiff white card, draw a circle with a diameter ½in (1.5cm) larger than your mirror. Cut this out and glue it onto thin wadding (batting) and, when dry, trim around the disc.

3 Position the stitched work over the padded disc. Snip the edges neatly into tabs and tape down on the other side. Glue the mirror over the taped edges.

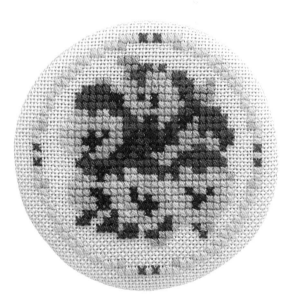

Needle Case

Turn a friend's zodiac sign into a useful gift.

* Black 28-count evenweave, 8 x 4½in (20 x 11cm)
* DMC stranded cottons (floss) as listed in the key
* Lining fabric, 8 x 4½in (20 x 11cm)
* Felt, 6 x 3in (16 x 8cm); cord

1 Orient the evenweave so that long edges are top and bottom. Stitch the selected zodiac motif from page 83 so that the border is 0in (0cm) from the right-hand edge.

2 Lay the felt on the right side of the lining fabric and sew the two together with a row of stitches down the centre. Lay this section felt-side-up and lay the embroidered rectangle on top with the stitching face down.

3 Sew a seam ½in (1cm) around the edges, leaving an opening for turning. Trim the corners, turn the case right side out and handsew the opening closed.

4 Tie a length of cord around the spine and trim ends.

STITCHING TECHNIQUES

Reading the Charts

In cross stitch, a motif is transferred from a charted design onto unmarked fabric. A key tells you which colour of DMC stranded cotton (floss) relates to which colour square on the relevant chart. Working the design is simply a matter of stitching a series of crosses in the appropriate colour according to the arrangement on the chart.

Many designs also include backstitch, shown on the chart as thick lines, and a few include French knots, shown as dots. Arrows indicate the centre of the design.

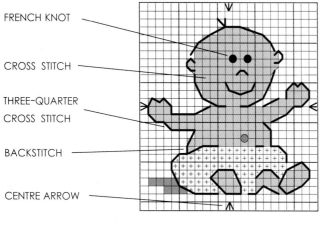

FRENCH KNOT

CROSS STITCH

THREE-QUARTER
CROSS STITCH

BACKSTITCH

CENTRE ARROW

Fabric

Cross stitch fabrics are evenly woven, that is, they have the same number of threads over a given distance both vertically and horizontally. Aida fabric, formed with bands of threads, is often used. Fabric woven in single threads can be made of various fibres but they're referred to in this book as evenweave. Fabrics for cross stitch are available in a wide range of colours.

The size of each stitch is determined by the number of fabric threads over which you sew and by the number of bands or threads per inch (known as the fabric count). 28-count evenweave has twenty-eight threads of fabric per inch and each cross stitch covers two threads (to prevent the embroidery thread gliding under a fabric thread) so there are fourteen stitches per inch.

The instructions for each project specify the type of fabric used to stitch it and the amount of fabric required. When you choose a fabric with a different thread count, you will need to calculate what the size of the stitched design will be. Use the following rule: finished size equals the design stitch count divided by the fabric count (and then divided by two if working with evenweave rather than Aida). Multiply the result by 2.5 to convert from inches into centimetres.

Thread & Equipment

All designs in this book have been stitched with DMC stranded cotton (floss). If you wish to use a different brand, match the colours in the pictures as closely as possible or create your own combinations afresh. A chart on page 104 offers a guide for converting to Anchor threads.

The six strands of the embroidery thread can be split into single strands, three lengths of double strands, or other combinations. All of the projects in this book are stitched with two strands for cross stitch and one for backstitch and French knots, unless specified in the project notes.

Use a blunt needle such as a small tapestry needle that will not split the fabric threads. A size 26 needle is suitable for all of the projects in this book.

You will need two pairs of scissors: a small pair for trimming threads and a pair of shears for cutting fabric.

Preparing to Stitch

Cut the fabric to size and locate the centre by folding the fabric piece in half and then in half again. When you start stitching, make sure the centre of the design (indicated by arrows on the chart) matches the centre point of your fabric. Orient the fabric shape to match the chart and count out from the centre point to where you want to start stitching.

Cut a length of embroidery thread, say 16in (40cm) long, and gently split it into the appropriate number of strands. Let the strands dangle and untwist.

Stitching

Thread the needle with the appropriate number of strands and bring it through the fabric, leaving ½in (1.5cm) of waste thread at the back. Hold this tail carefully and make sure that your first four or five stitches secure it, then trim any excess thread.

CROSS STITCH

Stitch a series of diagonal bars running from left to right. Then, at the end of the row, return by stitching the top bars from right to left. Drop your needle to the bottom of the next row and repeat the process.

The number of threads crossed by a single stitch will depend on your fabric: on evenweave, each stitch covers two threads, on Aida each stitch covers one band of threads.

Work horizontally rather than vertically and avoid changing directions; even though you may use more stranded cotton (floss), the result will look much neater.

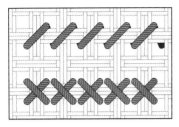

Working a row of cross stitches

Once you have stitched some crosses, use them as your reference point and count from them, rather than from the centre. Complete each colour block, jumping short distances where necessary, but always securing the thread at the back by running the needle under existing threads. If blocks are some distance apart, finish off the first and start afresh.

To finish off each section, run your needle through the back of four or five stitches and trim the stranded cotton (floss) close to the fabric.

THREE-QUARTER STITCH

Many of the charts contain some three-quarter stitches. These are indicated on the chart by a right-angled triangle and are usually found around the edges of a motif. In this case, one diagonal of the cross stitch is formed in the usual way, but the second stitch is brought down into the central hole of linen, or into the centre of an Aida block.

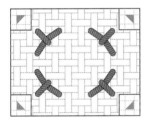

Where the chart indicates two different three-quarter stitches in the same square, you will need to decide which colour should dominate.

BACKSTITCH

Many of the charts include backstitch to define outlines and provide detail. It is shown as a solid line on the chart. Backstitch is always worked after the cross stitching is completed and is worked in a continuous line. The method is best shown in a diagram.

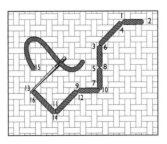

Backstitch can be worked as single stitches over one or two counts of fabric, or as longer stitches when working a cat's whisker or another such feature.

FRENCH KNOTS

These are useful stitches for adding tiny features such as eyes. In this book they are usually worked with a single strand of stranded cotton (floss) and are shown on the chart as a small coloured dot.

To work a French knot, bring the needle up to the right side of the fabric, hold the thread down with your left thumb (if you are right-handed) and wind the thread around the needle twice or three times, depending on the size of knot you want. Still holding the thread taut, push the needle through to the back of the work, one thread or a part of a band away from the entry point. See the diagrams below.

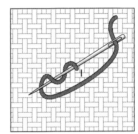 

Extra Tips

Keep your work as clean and fresh as possible. When not in use, secure the needle at the edge of the fabric to prevent rust marks or damage to the fabric.

As most of the designs are worked with two strands of stranded cotton (floss), here is a useful tip: cut a long single strand, thread both ends through the needle and catch the end loop at the back on your first stitch to secure the end.

As you stitch, the thread tends to twist. This may produce uneven stitches so, if it happens, let the needle dangle from the fabric so that the thread can unwind.

When moving from one area of a colour to another patch of the same colour, don't jump the thread too far across the back if the gap will remain bare. Such leaps will show through the fabric in the finished work.

If you make an error, do not try to rescue the embroidery thread for reuse. Use a pair of small pointed scissors to snip misplaced stitches and carefully pull out the strands. Then stitch correctly with new stranded cotton (floss).

Finishing

When stitching is complete, you can give the work a gentle wash in lukewarm water with a mild detergent. Rinse it well and place on a clean white towel to dry. To press, lay the work face down on a towel, cover it with a clean cloth and iron it gently. Check the work closely for unwanted filaments, front and back, before you mount it as a card.

MAKING CARDS

Once you've cross stitched your design, it's time to turn it into a greetings card. A wide range of pre-cut card mounts are available commercially but it's not difficult to make your own, following the instructions below. After that, it's simply a matter of mounting the cross stitch in the card and perhaps adding a little decorative touch.

Materials & Equipment

Apart from the materials you've used to cross stitch, there are a few bits and pieces that you'll need to finish the project. These are all readily available from craft shops, but you probably have most of them already. They are:

* scissors for cutting paper
* double-sided adhesive tape
* a cutting board
* a craft knife
* a ruler
* a set square
* a pair of compasses for drawing circles

Sheets of card can be bought in a delightful array of colours and textures. Card with a weight of about 220 gsm (gram per square metre) is ideal, but you might like to experiment. Packets of mixed card colours might be a good choice, but make sure the sheets are large enough to cut a double-fold card.

Handmade paper gives a very special effect, but can be difficult to cut neatly. Consider using it for a single-fold card and tearing the edges, rather than cutting them.

Making Tags

A gift tag can be a simple scrap of card with a piece of stitched fabric stuck on, or it can be a small version of a greetings card and take the single- or double-fold format. All kinds can be bought ready-made, or you can make your own by cutting a shape and punching a hole in one corner, or by following the directions below, but on a small scale.

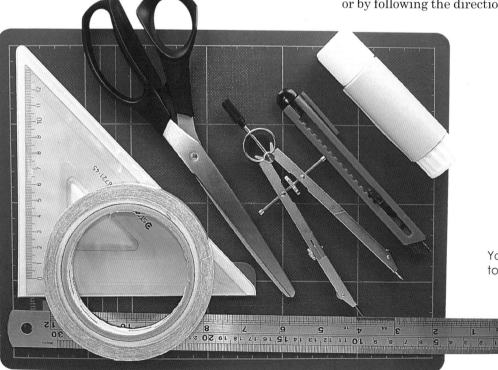

You only need a few items to make cards.

A double-fold (right) has three panels and a window cut in the middle panel.

A single fold card (below) has only two panels and no window.

Single-fold Cards

The most basic card is a single-fold card, with a fold running either along the side or the top. To make one, decide how large you want the card front to be and then double either the width or height, depending on where the fold will be.

Mark a rectangle this size on a sheet of card using a ruler and a set square, and rule a pencil line dividing it in two along the proposed fold. Cut out the shape with a sharp knife and then run the knife very lightly along the fold line, scoring the card so it folds neatly. If the edges don't meet when the card is folded, trim to neaten.

Trim the stitched fabric and fringe the edges neatly. Stick strips of double-sided tape onto the back of the stitched fabric, position it carefully on the front of the card and then press it firmly in place.

Double-fold Cards

A double-fold card has three panels with a window in the middle panel in which to frame the cross stitch. The most common shapes for windows are square, rectangular, oval and circular, but you can create any shape you like.

A speedy approach is to use a bought pre-cut card as a template for cutting your own. Alternatively, create your own range of paper templates and keep them for cutting future cards. A home computer would be a good tool for this: you could use basic drawing software to create shapes and use print-outs as templates for cutting the card.

Remember, if your sheet of card is not large enough, you can always cut a single-fold card with a window in the front and back it with a separate panel of card.

MEASURING & MARKING

A particular size and shape of window is recommended for each project displayed in a double-fold card. Decide what size the front of the finished card will be, allowing space around the window. For a card that has the fold at the side, multiply the width by three. For a card with the fold at the top, multiply the height by three.

Using a ruler, set square and pencil, mark the card outline as a rectangle on a sheet of card. Measure and mark two lines to divide the rectangle into three equal panels. Take care to get the angles right or the edges of the folded card won't meet.

On the middle panel, mark the window. The easiest way to do this is to cut out a paper template for the window, position it on the card and then draw around it: this is particulary sensible if the window is an unusual shape. A couple of projects in this book require an irregular-shaped window; trace the patterns on page 102 and make paper templates for these. The best effect is often achieved if you allow a little more space below the window than above.

CUTTING

Using a sharp craft knife, a cutting mat and a ruler, cut out the complete card shape. On the outside of the card, run the craft knife very lightly along the two fold lines: these scored lines should now fold cleanly.

Cut out the window using a ruler as a guide for any straight lines. For a curved shape, you will need a little patience and a steady hand. Don't throw away the cutout window: it will make a nice tag for another project.

Finally, you will need to trim a narrow strip off the edge of the backing panel, so that the card will close neatly.

If you're using a pre-cut card in a landscape fashion (that is, with the fold at the top), you might need to trim a little off the right-hand edge to ensure the window is centred.

The inside of this double-fold card has backing paper in place and strips of double-sided tape in position.

MOUNTING

First, identify which is the top of your open card and which is the backing panel; it's surprisingly easy to find you've mounted your stitching upside down. Now trim the stitched fabric so that it will fit inside the card once it is folded; make sure it remains larger than the window.

If the fabric used is a contrasting colour to that of the card, it is often a good idea to stick a piece of paper on the inside of the backing panel. This is particularly important if you have used a pale fabric and a dark card, as the cross stitch word can look muddied without a backing; in this case you'd use a white piece of paper. Make sure you glue it onto the correct panel.

On the inside of the middle panel, stick strips of double-sided tape around the window; if the window is curved, cut the tape into small pieces. Peel off any tape backing.

Place the stitching face up on a clean surface and open up the card so that you can see the design through the window. Carefully position the design in the window and then press the card down onto the fabric.

Place strips of double-sided tape along the three outside edges of the backing panel, fold over the panel and press it down firmly. Your work should now appear in the window.

ADDING A DOUBLE MOUNT

Picture framers often make use of a double mount to make a greater statement and it's only a little trouble for the card maker to do the same. Of course, you need to decide this before you mount the work.

Choose a piece of card in a contrasting colour to the card body (perhaps matching one of the thread colours in the design) and cut a piece slightly smaller than the front of the card. Mark a shape that is ¼in (5mm) smaller all around than the main window and cut it out with a craft knife. As a first step in the mounting procedure above, glue this double-mount inside the middle panel of the card.

You can use a variation of this idea if the design you have stitched doesn't fill the window of an available card. The engagement card on page 52 makes good use of coloured strips along the top and bottom of the window.

Decorating Cards

It may be that your cross stitch card needs no further embellishment. If, however, it looks a little understated, or there are large blank areas, try adding some interest with the following ideas.

EMBOSSING

An attractive feature of many pre-cut cards is the embossed line around the window. If you're cutting your own cards,

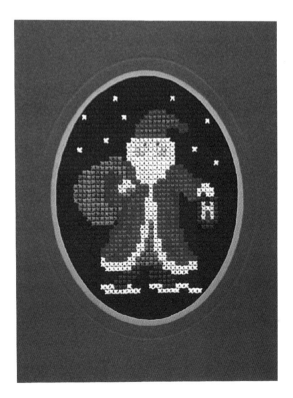

The double mount in a contrasting colour adds an elegant finish to this card.

Keep a box of items for decorating your finished cards.

it's easy to add this feature, especially if the window is square or rectangular. Lay a ruler so that its edge is ¼in (5mm) off the edge of the window and run the back of a sharp-tipped knife over the card, extending the line ¼in (5mm) beyond the window, so that your other embossed lines will meet neatly.

To emboss around a circular window, find a drinking glass with a rim slightly larger than the window, place it upside down over the window and run the back of the knife around this. An oval window is tricky: you'll need to pencil a line around the window and then emboss freehand!

OUTLINING

A gold or silver outline around the window adds a little class to a card and is especially easy if the card mount has an embossed line already. Choose a fine-nibbed pen and shake it well, then use a ruler as a guide, or work freehand around a curve, to draw a neat line about ¼in (5mm) outside of the window.

For a circular window, use a pair of compasses to first draw a pencil line and then go over it with a metallic pen.

BITS & BOBS

Any number of small items can be stuck onto the front of a card, as long as it will fit into an envelope. Be careful, though, not to overwhelm your cross stitching; anything extra is supposed to add rather than detract from it.

Some possible additions are:

* small beads   * buttons
* adhesive stars   * glitter glue
* ribbon strips or bows * small paper shapes
* sequins

Another idea is to use a gold or silver pen to draw small swirls, stars or other squiggles, such as the pawprints shown on page 59.

The cards pictured have been given the finishing touch with a gold outline (left), embossing (middle), and gold leaves (right).

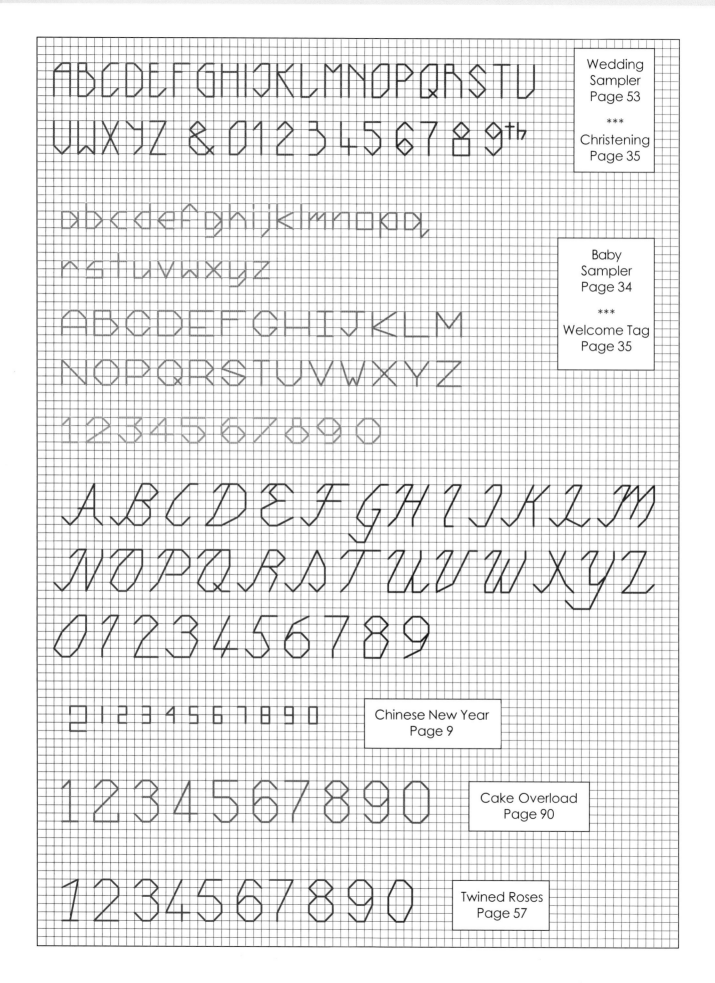

Wedding Sampler Page 53

***

Christening Page 35

Baby Sampler Page 34

***

Welcome Tag Page 35

Chinese New Year Page 9

Cake Overload Page 90

Twined Roses Page 57

Driving Test
Page 51

Hogmanay
Page 8

Hippos
Page 89

Fruit Tree
Page 90

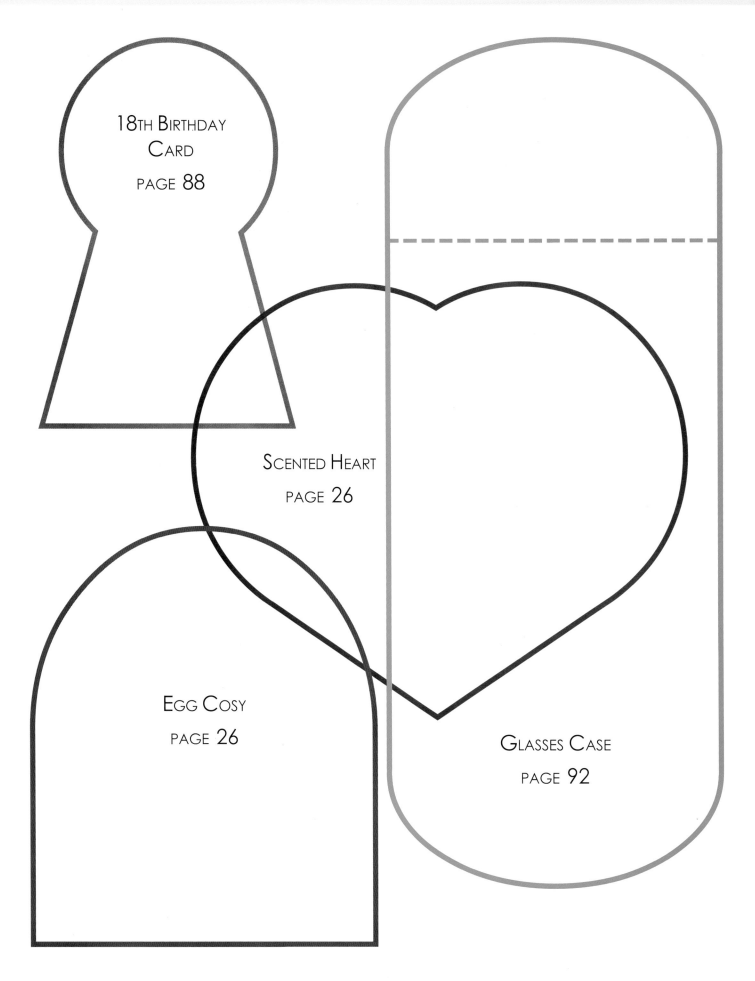

18TH BIRTHDAY
CARD
PAGE 88

SCENTED HEART
PAGE 26

EGG COSY
PAGE 26

GLASSES CASE
PAGE 92

United Kingdom

DMC CREATIVE WORLD LTD
Pullman Road, Wigston, Leicester, LE8 2DY
Tel: 0116 281 1040
Cross stitch fabrics and stranded cottons.

IMPRESS CARDS & CRAFT MATERIALS
Slough Farm, Westhall,
Halesworth, Suffolk, IP19 8RN
Tel: 01986 781422
Fax: 01986 781677
Email: sales@impresscards.co.uk
www.impresscards.com
Blank card mounts.

CRAFT CREATIONS LTD
Ingersoll House, Delamare Rd,
Cheshunt, Hertfordshire, EN8 9HD
Tel: 01992 781900
Fax: 01992 634339
Email: enquiries@craftcreations.com
www.craftcreations.com
Blank cards and cardmaking supplies.

SEW AND SO
Tel: 01453 752022
www.sewandso.co.uk
*Cross stitch fabrics, stranded cottons
and accessories.*

USA

THE DMC CORPORATION
Port Kearney Bld, 10 South Kearney, NJ
070732-0650
www.dmc-usa.com
Cross stitch fabrics and stranded cottons.

CHARLES CRAFT
PO Box 1049, Laurinburg, NC 28352
Tel: 910 844 3521
www.charlescraft.com
Cross stitch fabrics and accessories.

Australia

RADDA PTY LTD
PO Box 317, Earlwood NSW 2206
Tel: 02 9559 3088
Distributors of DMC stranded cottons.

IRELAND NEEDLECRAFT PTY LTD
PO Box 1175, Narre Warren MDC Vic 3805
Tel: 03 9702 3222
www.irelandneedlecraft.com.au
*Cross stitch fabrics, stranded cottons and
accessories.*

STADIA PTY LTD
PO Box 281, Paddington NSW 2021
Tel: 02 9328 7900
www.stadia.com.au
*Cross stitch fabrics, stranded cottons and
accessories.*

Charting Software

The designs in this book were created using
StitchCraft, an excellent Windows-based
software program. For information on this
program, please contact:
CRAFTED SOFTWARE
PO Box 78, Wentworth Falls NSW 2782
Australia
Tel: 61 2 4757 3136
Email: mail@stitchcraft.com.au
www.stitchcraft.com.au

Thanks!

Thank you to Radda for DMC cottons,
to Impress Cards for blank card mounts and
to Crafted Software for ongoing support.

DMC stranded cotton (floss) has been used to stitch the designs in this book.
If you wish to use the Anchor brand, refer to this chart for the equivalent
*shades. An * indicates that the Anchor shade has been used more than once.*

DMC	ANCHOR	DMC	ANCHOR	DMC	ANCHOR	DMC	ANCHOR	DMC	ANCHOR
151	73	550	101*	793	176*	995	410*	3825	323*
153	95	552	99	794	175	996	433	3826	1049*
155	1030	553	98	798	146	3012	855	3827	311*
156	118*	554	95	799	145	3013	853	3831	29
157	120*	562	210	807	168	3021	905	3837	100
159	120*	581	281	809	130	3022	8581*	3838	177
164	240	597	1064	814	45	3024	388	3839	176*
165	278*	603	62	816	43	3078	292	3840	120*
166	280	604	55	817	13*	3326	36	3841	159
208	110	605	1094	822	390	3328	1024	3843	1089*
209	109	606	334	838	1088	3340	329	3844	410*
210	108	608	330	839	1086	3341	328	3845	1089*
211	342	646	8581*	841	1082	3347	266*	3846	1090
301	1049*	647	1040	898	380	3348	264	3848	1074*
304	19	648	900	904	258	3364	261	3849	1070*
307	289	666	46	905	257	3607	87	3851	186*
310	403	677	361*	906	256*	3608	86	3853	1003*
317	400	699	923*	907	255	3609	85	3854	313
318	235*	700	228	909	923*	3706	33	3855	311*
321	47	701	227	910	230	3708	31	3856	347
340	118*	702	226	911	205	3712	1023	3863	379
341	117	703	238	912	209	3713	1020	3865	2
349	13*	704	256*	913	204	3716	25	5283	—
350	11	718	88	917	89	3747	120	5284	—
351	10	720	326	918	341	3753	1031	ecru	387*
352	9	721	324	920	1004	3755	140	blanc	1
353	8*	722	323*	921	1003*	3756	1037		
355	1014	725	305	928	274	3761	928		
369	1043	726	295*	946	332	3765	170		
371	887	727	293	948	1011	3766	167		
400	351	728	306*	951	1010	3770	1009		
402	1047	729	890	954	203*	3776	1048*		
413	236*	738	361*	955	203*	3777	1015		
414	235*	739	366	958	187	3781	1050		
415	398	740	316	959	186*	3787	904		
422	372	741	304	963	23	3799	236*		
434	310	742	303	964	185	3801	1098		
435	365	743	302	967	6	3807	122		
436	363	744	301	972	298	3810	1066		
437	362	745	300	973	290	3811	1060		
444	291	747	158	975	357	3812	188		
451	233	760	1022	976	1001	3814	1074		
452	232	761	1021	977	1002	3816	876		
453	231	762	234	986	246	3819	278*		
470	266*	772	259	987	244	3820	306*		
471	265	775	128	988	243	3822	295*		
472	253	782	308	989	242	3823	386		
535	401	792	941	993	1070*	3824	8*		

INDEX